DON'T SHOOT THE BASTARDS (YET)

101 More Ways to Salvage Freedom

by Claire Wolfe

Loompanics Unlimited
Port Townsend, Washington

This book is sold for informational purposes only. Neither the author nor the publisher will be held accountable for the use or misuse of the information contained in this book.

Don't Shoot The Bastards (Yet): 101 More Ways to Salvage Freedom
© 1999 by Claire Wolfe

Published by:
Loompanics Unlimited
P.O. Box 1197
Port Townsend, WA 98368
Loompanics Unlimited is a division of Loompanics Enterprises, Inc.
1-360-385-2230
E-mail: loompanx@olympus.net
Web site: www.loompanics.com

Cover art by Jim Blanchard

ISBN 1-55950-189-8
Library of Congress Card Catalog 98-89027

Table of Contents

To
Walter (Wat) Tyler
d. 1381

Just another damned troublemaking peasant
who trusted a king.

We are all outlaws in the eyes of America....
We are forces of chaos and anarchy
Everything they say we are we are
And we are very
Proud of ourselves
— Jefferson Airplane, *"We Can Be Together"*

Acknowledgments

The following friends, acquaintances and correspondents contributed to this book: Carl Alexander, Charles Curley, Jim Davidson, Dave Dawson, Marc Donais, Mike Dugger, Bill Evans, Leon Felkins, Genevieve Gray, John Greenley, Michael Harries, Woody Hassler, Hobbit, Wayne Dennis Holt, J.J. Johnson, Dennis Justice, Mike Kemp, Bob Kephart, Tim Kern, David B. King, Alan Korwin, Don Lynch, Victor Milan, K.J. Miller, Patricia Neill, Eric Oppen, Cyndee Parker, Ken Royce, Sherwood Schantz, L. Neil Smith, Brian Stedjee, K. Parker Stoops, Vin Suprynowicz, Ed "No Relation to Claire" Wolfe, and Carl Worden. Lots of people also e-mailed quotes which I've used throughout the book; thanks to you all!

The following strangers, and others, contributed through their Web sites, written works or personal examples: Shirley Allen, Monica Cellio (whose Web site provided a gold mine of quotes), Paul B. Dennis, John Q. Newman, John Pugsley, Gene Sharp, Stevyn and the *Iron Feather Journal*, the late Robert Shea, J.D. Tuccille, Robert Anton Wilson, and the hysterically paranoid officials of Washington state and Indiana.

Finally, all credit to the Loompanics crew: Mike Hoy, the Big Boss; Vanessa McGrady, master publicist; Richard Voss, Marketing Coordinator; Jay Vee, computer guru; Jan, who makes my books look good; Lou, who catches my mistakes; Audrey, without whom the wheels would stop turning; and all the members of the world's fastest and most efficient shipping department.

Being mentioned here does not imply even the slightest degree of agreement with my ideas. Though many people helped with the good stuff, all mistakes, dumb opinions and rash statements are strictly my own.

Introduction
by Boston T. Party

In the arena of ideas women have historically fought mightily alongside men. Throughout the 20th century's struggle for the quality of Liberty won by the Revolutionary War, it has been our fortune to have experienced the chromatic female mind of certain women who joined the literary fray. The names of Rose Wilder Lane (*The Discovery of Freedom*), Isabel Paterson (*The God of the Machine*), Ayn Rand (*Atlas Shrugged*, etc.), Taylor Caldwell (*Devil's Advocate*, etc.), and Wendy McElroy are probably already well-known and loved by many of you.

To the above I would add the name of Claire Wolfe. I'm sure you'll agree after reading **Don't Shoot the Bastards (Yet): 101 More Ways to Salvage Freedom.**

When I read her first book, *101 Things To Do 'Til The Revolution*, I was knocked out of my mind's chair. There was something fresh and well-seasoned! Her line, "America is at that awkward stage. It's too late to work within the system, but too early to shoot the bastards" is undoubtedly the very best summation of Liberty's predicament, and is destined to join the ranks of immortal quotes, such as Jefferson's "...tree of liberty..." and Henry's "or give me death." She encapsulated many of my own thoughts and conclusions, and to read them in somebody else's book was simultaneously gratifying and... eerie.

Less personally put, I think she's on to something. She has grasped the current stage of our struggle: firm mental defiance coupled with the beginning of real action.

One of my goals as an author is to create more of a synthesis between Conservative Republicans, Libertarians, and Patriots (who lean towards Populism). In a nutshell, I'd like the Patriots to grow some brains, the Libertarians to grow a gonad, and the Conservative Republicans to grow both. Those of us who profess to love freedom are probably in roughly 75 percent agreement, yet we fight over the remaining 25 percent (which are moot items unless we achieve political power). I get the sense that Claire Wolfe is also trying to meld such a synthesis.

Libertarians, for example, are divided into two camps, which I've named "Egghead Libs" and "Action Libs." Over their Manhattan quiche, Egghead Libs endlessly ponder the philosophical immorality of coercive taxation to pay for urban rat control in Newark, etc., etc., etc. Truly, it has reached the point of intellectual masturbation. They are like Franciscan monks pontificating whether or not Jesus owned the cloak on his back, instead of actively evangelizing the Gospel. Instead of embracing, or at least blandly supporting, the modern movements of un-taxation, sovereign citizenship, and militias, the Egghead Libs very plainly distanced themselves from all that "rabble."

I think Egghead Libs secretly know (or at least suspect) that they'll never be hosting an Inaugural Ball, and therefore constrain the urgent business of Freedom to mere thought and word. They have perfectly dressed a mannequin of Liberty with the splendid attire of Rand and Rothbard (or,

---

the black leather of Spooner and Nock for that "bad ass" look). They even go so far as to carry on conversations with it in the form of cybercommunities and other schemes of "Virtual Freedom" (my term). It all reminds me of children playing "Hospital" — it's great fun, but at the avoidance of real issues of Life and Death. (Note: I've nothing inherently against cyberlibs. In fact, I've been tinkering with my own ideas on Virtual Freedom. Although it's fine to have one's frothy little head in the clouds, one's feet are best left on the hard ground of Reality.)

My point here is that thought (in political context) is a means to the end of action, and most freedom activists have forsaken the cold, tough environment of action for the warm, safe bed of thought. This explains why they are not feared (and hardly noticed) by the DemoPublicans and Corporate Fascists. People all snugly under their bedcovers are no threat to anyone.

Exhibit A: At a 1997 Colorado Libertarian Party convention, a women's panel explored why the party did not attract many women. Although the replies from the dozen or so ladies were resoundingly tactful and sweetly diplomatic, the truth was, however, clearly audible to all present: Libertarian men are usually wimps. Conclusion: Lady Libs are looking for Action Lib men.

Exhibit B: At a recent Libertarian gathering, one of the keynote speakers (a veritable giant in the Libertarian movement) waxed beatifically about how technology was going to save our freedoms. He posed the hypothetical example of ringing every convicted felon's ankle with a locating device which was tracked in real-time by satellites. Then, whenever a mugging occurs the police can simply round up for a witness lineup all the Bad Guys shown to have been in that area during the assault. While the room nodded their agreement, I blew an O-ring. "Hey Charles, why not carry a gun and shoot the mugger?" About a third of the attendees chuckled/laughed/clapped, and the rest sat there in silence, horrified. (Charles stammered that he'd take questions at the end of his talk. I walked out muttering something about delay being the deadliest form of denial.)

Claire Wolfe — Action Lib — would have stood on her chair, whistling. Action Libs had their Egghead stage, and grew out of it. They understand that Liberty is a rough business, never completed, and ultimately requires, after some Point Of No Return, the resolution of armed defiance and a few deciliters of spilled blood. There has never been any other way to prune tyranny, and there never will be. PGP and cybermoney are fine tools to enhance Liberty, but they are no substitute for the well sorted-out, righteously indignant, locked-and-loaded American who proclaims "No further!" Ms. Wolfe not only knows that down to her Jeffersonian socks, but has the "embarrassing temerity" to loudly proclaim such far and wide.

During the years of the Berlin Wall, one East Berliner quipped, "Everybody has his bags packed mentally, but nobody is doing anything more than talk." Claire Wolfe is through with merely talking about her "packed bags" for the promised land of Galt's Gulch, and is coloring in the road map while her Caspar Milquetoast compatriots wrestle over such burning issues as Bastiat: Objectivist or Libertarian? Her books are a long overdue slap in their face, and command of "Oh, shut up and get in the car!"

Don't Shoot The Bastards (Yet) just might reach the Randus Invertebratus. For those of you actually sporting a backbone, you'll likely find your good posture further improved by her words, which somehow manage to simultaneously be fun and serious. Early bits, such as using J. Edgar Hoover's Social Security number as your own and wearing garlic at your next IRS audit, provide sorely needed laughs during these mirthless times. Item #26 sheds great insight to the paranoia of law (edict) enforcement. Given that I am an incorrigible firebrand, my favorite part of this hearty collection of ascending resolve is found, predictably, towards the end ("...dealing with nasty times and nasty people"), and this is where Ms. Wolfe shines. (Items #93, #99, and #101 are, for example, among the book's finest gems.) It's easy to make a reader chuckle loudly or ponder deeply, but her book made me do both — and that's what makes it such a joy.

A male admirer of Ayn Rand once called her "a very courageous man" — to her stunned delight. I would apply this compliment to Claire Wolfe, as she is one of the bravest men I know. We are very fortunate indeed to have such a clear, practical voice so late in the game when Tyranny, supported by Cowards and Fools, once again reigns over the Free and the Brave.

Note: Boston T. Party is the trademarked *nom de plume* of Kenneth W. Royce, author of *Good-Bye April 15th!*, *You & The Police!*, *Bulletproof Privacy*, *Hologram of Liberty*, and *Boston's Gun Bible* — most of which are available through Loompanics. He may be reached (sort of) via www.javelinpress.com.

Preface

Tyrants refuse to understand that some of us are free. Not that we will fight for freedom or wish for freedom, or petition for freedom. But that we will simply *be* free no matter what they do. They can kill us — a cheap and ultimately ineffective tactic. But they will never make that troublesome, chaotic, uncontrollable thing — freedom — go away. It will always buzz around their heads like an annoying insect. And someday that flighty little bug might sting them.

We are that tiny, yet powerful creature. We are the minority of the human race that is drawn to the shining vision of freedom and who will live by no other light. We are few in numbers. We probably always will be. But tyrants make a grave error when they fail to realize the power of our passion.

If you value freedom that much, this book is for you. If you don't (yet) value freedom that much, but feel a stirring toward freedom's light, read on. If you love freedom, but are coming to the conclusion you've been looking for it in the wrong place or the wrong way, you are especially welcome.

If you don't love freedom, if what you love is control, then understand this. We will be free. And if you try to halt our flight, we will sting you.

What this book is

This is a follow-up to my earlier book, *101 Things to Do 'Til the Revolution*. It covers the same themes — self-liberation, monkeywrenching and preparedness — but contains all new material. Like the earlier book, it is for action-oriented people, not those who want to remain in ivory towers, and not those who want to remain quiet and well-behaved as they beg others to win freedom for them. It contains 101 different items to think about or (if you are so inclined) to act upon, or to use as inspiration for even better ideas of your own.

In addition to having all new material, it's different from *101 Things* in two important ways:

- It is more hard-core in two areas. *101 Things* recommended a lot of general reading matter on the subject of freedom. With few exceptions, any books mentioned in this volume are strictly action-oriented. Also, *101 Things* noted a number of political groups worth joining. As I explain in Item 13, I no longer believe in promoting advocacy groups of any stripe. Direct action is the thing.

- While *101 Things* was almost randomly arranged, with this book I've at least nodded in the direction of order. It begins with gentler and more philosophical items and gradually moves on to those requiring more hard-core conviction. That's the general approach, anyway. However, if my gut told me an item belonged *right there*, I put it right there, regardless of how hard-core or philosophical it might be.

If you have read the original *101 Things*, you might want to know that it is still being continuously updated with new addresses, phone numbers, Web sites and e-mail addresses added at each printing. Items that become obsolete are

---

replaced. That book is still very much alive and continues to be a work in progress.

But the book you're holding in your hands is a separate work. You don't have to have read *101 Things* to read this one. If you have read *101 Things*, most of this book will still be new to you.

Is it time?

101 Things opened with words that have since become famous as an e-mail signature line and a definition of a freedom-lover's dilemma: "America is at that awkward stage. It's too late to work within the system, but too early to shoot the bastards." For what it's worth (and I get asked all the time), I still think it's too early. In fact, I hope devoutly that we never have to shoot anybody to be free. But I do believe that, since I wrote those words, we have moved on to a new stage in the passion for freedom — one that requires more creativity and may require more ruthlessness than we good people are ready for.

Any revolution will be, I hope, a revolution of the heart and of life choices, not of violence. But let's be realistic. If governments continue their relentless assault on freedom, and if they don't simply allow us free ones to depart, peacefully, from their control, one day we'll have to choose between shooting and slavery. It is a day to be dreaded and avoided. But if it comes, may we have the sense and the grace to recognize it and to do the right thing.

This book doesn't advocate initiating violence against anyone, at any time. Very much the contrary. But it does advocate taking back stolen freedom and making those who take it from us learn that tyranny does not pay. We must. That is a given of being human and fully alive.

My opinions

I often state strong opinions. But keep in mind that opinions are what they are. No matter how forcefully I express myself, my thoughts have no power over anyone. I've said it before, but I can't say it loudly enough: Anyone who acts, based solely on the ideas or urgings of others, is a colossal, damned fool, incapable of truly understanding or exercising freedom. Please don't be one! Think for yourself and act *solely* on your own wisdom.

If something in this book looks like a bright idea to you, investigate the ramifications *for yourself* before acting upon it — particularly if it's anything that could be risky. If something in this book looks like the sheerest block-headedness to you, then call me a blockhead — and go do something different. Remember that, contrary to received opinion, no one becomes an "expert" simply by writing a book. And even if I were a renowned expert in a thousand things, there is one thing about which you are infinitely more expert than any expert on the planet — living your own life. So take the contents of this book, as the publisher says, For Informational Purposes Only. Do nothing but what your own mind, common sense and conscience tell you is right.

I hope every reader will learn something worthwhile within these pages. But even if you simply learn what you *don't* want to do, you may have gained something.

The important thing is to *act* for freedom, and to act freely. Your way may be different from mine. Isn't that the definition of freedom, after all? The only tragedy would be if passionate, intelligent lovers of freedom failed to act at all.

Chapter One

In which we begin nice and easy. We lay some ground-work, ruminate upon mindset, and indulge in modest measures of philosophical maundering, with only a hint of risky business.

1. Question fundamentals

- Why does the government, rather than insurance companies or driving schools, issue driver certifications?

- Why was the federal government created — and who created it?

- If your house and land actually belong to you, how can your local government threaten to take them away simply because you refuse to pay them money each year?

- How can something be a government agency and a "corporation" at the same time?

- How can a government agency claim to protect the "interests of all" when it is making profits, in the form of royalties, off corporations' products? (As the USDA is now doing with Monsanto's genetically altered "terminator" seed?)

- Why is the "news" that happens in Washington or that is reported from New York more important to you than the news that happens in your own neighborhood and town?

- If government lands actually belong to you and your neighbors, then how come you and your neighbors don't have any control over how they're used?

- If you tried to fight General Motors in a court paid for by General Motors, before a judge and prosecutors whose livelihood depended entirely on General Motors, no one would imagine you could get a fair trial. Why would anyone imagine you could get a fair trial in a tax-paid court when your problem is with the tax-paying system?

- What does "taxation without representation" mean?

- Where did the Federal Communications Commission get the authority to levy taxes — as it now does via a special assessment on your phone bill?

- Where did the federal government acquire authority to set up: The FBI? The Department of Education? The Bureau of Alcohol, Tobacco and Firearms?

- Who wrote the Pledge of Allegiance, and why?

- Churches, being 501(c)(3) tax-exempt organizations, are forbidden to engage in political activity. So how come a big, mainstream church like the Presbyterians can lobby, year after year, for more government (gun control; social programs), while a little church that fights for less government (abolition of the IRS) loses its tax-exempt status?

- Why, if all you want to track is parents who are behind in their child support, do you set up a database to track every employed person in the country?

- Why did legislation implementing a "free trade agreement" (GATT) include a requirement that every infant in the country be given a Citizen ID Number at birth?

- If the country got along for more than 130 years without an income tax, why couldn't it do so again?

- If two world wars, a depression, a welfare state, a drug war and a burgeoning police state followed implementation of an income tax, might some of these not possibly be signs that an income tax is a bad idea?

- If education must be provided by the government because everyone needs education, why doesn't the government manufacture shoes? Refrigerators? Gasoline?

Don't start with the details. You will get lost in them and be ineffective. Question the fundamentals. Investigate "received truths." Be suspicious of the things "everybody knows."

H.L. Mencken once called American politics a "carnival of buncombe," and it is certainly that. Congress seems to want to cure every ill known to man except unconstitutional government and high taxes. Whenever anything makes headlines or hits the TV news-entertainment shows, some congressman or senator proposes a law. Pretty soon, they will have to build a monstrous new building just to house the federal statutes and federal regulations. — Charley Reese, syndicated columnist

2. A correspondent observes the law

A correspondent who prefers not to be credited wrote with an interesting observation about the nature and consequences of law-making:

> I was talking to my brother the other day about the "law maker" problem. I pointed out that, since freedom is having the option to choose either to do, or not do, some activity, that *every* law destroys freedom. That is because every law negates some option. My brother's comment was that we should start calling "law makers" what they really are — freedom destroyers.
>
> After the aforementioned discussion we arrived at what seems to be the root of the problem with our lunatic government. In the old days, laws were passed to punish people who had deliberately harmed others. But today laws are being passed to punish people for *being able* to harm others. "You can't own that gun because you *could* use it to inflict harm." But such laws are totally arbitrary because everyone (except helpless infants) *could* harm others. And every technological device ever invented *could* be used to harm others. And all knowledge of how to build potentially harmful technological devices *could* be used to cause harm. The politicians — freedom destroyers — have begun a process that will eventually lead to the outlawing of everything that differentiates us from animals. It's back to the caves for us! And by the way, the knowledge of how to start fire will also have to be outlawed. Fire *could* be dangerous.

Politicians could be the most dangerous thing of all. Whatever shall we do with them?

> *To want to improve the situation of another human being presupposes an insight into his circumstances such as not even a poet has toward a character he himself has created. How much less insight is there in the so infinitely excluded helper... Wanting to change or improve someone's situation means offering him, in*

---

exchange for difficulties in which he is practiced and experienced, other difficulties that will perhaps find him even more bewildered. — Rainer Maria Rilke

3. A small rant about the nature of office holders

A "Bizarro" cartoon depicts a slick politician in suit-and-tie greeting lunchbucket guys filing out of a factory gate. The politician extends his hand and chirps:

> ...Hello there, I have the need to dominate, vote for me next Tuesday...Hi, I'd appreciate your vote, I define my worth by the approval of others...Hello, I'll tell you anything you want to hear if you'll vote for me...Hi there, I sure would like to push you around for a few years, vote for me next Tuesday...

A friend added a caption:

> If politicians had to tell the truth, this is what they'd be saying.

And don't you recognize a cosmic truth when you see it? The key to understanding politicians is to grasp that they are fundamentally sick people. Not strong. Not wise. Not inherently more capable than others. They are merely gripped by a desire, nay a desperation, to dominate others and dress their own egos in the emperor's clothes of power. Knowing this can help you eliminate your dependence upon them. If you knew that a person had a mental warpage that made him incapable of respecting the rights of others, would you keep throwing rational arguments for rights at him? Would you keep believing you had some duty to obey him? No, you'd just stay out of his way as best you could. Staying out of the way of criminal maniacs is difficult in a world gone mad with government. But it may also be your only sensible strategy for the moment.

Crime does not pay unless you get elected. — Andrew J. Galambos

4. Government supremacist: the power of words

Orwell knew that the struggle between freedom and tyranny was in part a struggle of language. The side that defines the terms defines the battlefield and selects the weapons. When professional victim disarmers got phrases like "gun violence" and "assault weapon" firmly embedded in the media, they gained a huge advantage because the disarmers now control how the general public *thinks* about firearms.

We must stop using the terminology favored by power lovers — which we sometimes do simply because their words have become so embedded in the language that we might not be able to think of any graceful alternatives. (How often, for instance, have you used the word "entitlements," even when you hate it?) We should speak the language of freedom, and do it in such a way that we make it clear we expect all sensible people to agree with us. Even if individuals don't agree, we are helping establish certain assumptions.

For instance:

It's not "public schools." It's *government* schools.

The government isn't "us." It's *them*. The federals. Washington, D.C.

It isn't "gun control." It's victim disarmament. Or disarmament of the innocent. Or disarmament of women.

They aren't our "representatives." They are "politicians" — which everyone knows is a dirty word. Or (with your voice dripping with sarcasm) they are our *rulers*, our *bosses*.

We don't obey laws. We're subject to *edicts*.

They aren't law enforcement officers. They're *enforcers*.

Those who want government to solve all problems are *government supremacists*.

It's not "taxation." It's *confiscation*.

It's *voluntary*, of course. (Get out that sarcasm again.)

It's not "Social Security." It's *insecurity*. Perhaps even *socialist insecurity*. The Ponzi retirement scheme.

They aren't feminists. They're *victim feminists* or *big-government feminists*.

It's not an entitlement. It's a *giveaway*.

It's not affirmative action. It's *affirmative apartheid.*[1] Sure, one is designed to favor whites & separate races, while the other is designed to favor Blacks & Hispanics and push races together.. But both are equally racist and equally loathsome as top-down social engineering.

And the latest self-help book? Why, it's *People Who Love Government Too Much* — a long overdue answer to one of America's most pressing problems!

> *The evils of tyranny are rarely seen but by him who resists it.* — John Hay, *"Castilian Days, II"*, 1872

5. The good (albeit dead) side of Marbury v. Madison

Very early on, specifically, in 1803, the U.S. Supreme Court gave us one of the best and one of the worst decisions in its history. They were actually the same decision, in the case of *Marbury v. Madison*. The ugly side of *Marbury* was the decision by those elitists that they, and they alone, had

---

[1] Thank you, Charles Curley, for the term "affirmative apartheid." "Victim disarmament" was a conscious invention of Dr. Morgan Reynolds and W.W. Caruth III, writing for the National Center for Policy Analysis. I first saw "government supremacist" in the e-zine, the *Vigo Examiner*.

the final say over whether a law was, or wasn't constitutional. Until that time, it had been an open question as to who would determine constitutionality. (See "Listen up, you state governments!!!" Item 9.) The good side of *Marbury* lies in the oft quoted declaration: "A law repugnant to the constitution is void" and it therefore merits no obedience from the day it takes effect. Unfortunately, the country has embraced the ugly *Marbury*, while the good side of *Marbury* has become a historical curiosity, important only to constitutionalists and other freedom lovers desperately seeking ways to curb burgeoning federal power.

Do you have to obey bad laws? Are trial judges and bureaucrats right to roll their eyes and tell you to take your silly little constitutional arguments elsewhere — which is what they usually do, these days? Should you await pronouncements from on high before deciding what's right and what isn't, under American law? Not according to some of America's original elitists.

Here's an extended quote from *Marbury*. The entire text concerning the invalidity of unconstitutional laws is such a gem I urge you to read it for yourself at www.laws.findlaw.com/US/5/137.html. Please especially note that the ancient Supremes considered this an *easy and obvious* decision!

> The question, whether an act, repugnant to the constitution, can become the law of the land, is a question deeply interesting to the United States; but, happily, not of an intricacy proportioned to its interest. It seems only necessary to recognize certain principles, supposed to have been long and well established, to decide it.

> That the people have an original right to establish, for their future government, such principles as, in their opinion, shall most conduce to their own happiness, is the basis on which the whole American fabric has been erected. The ex-

ercise of this original right is a very great exertion; nor can it nor ought it to be frequently repeated. The principles, therefore, so established are deemed fundamental. And as the authority, from which they proceed, is supreme, and can seldom act, they are designed to be permanent.

This original and supreme will organizes the government, and assigns to different departments their respective powers. It may either stop here; or establish certain limits not to be transcended by those departments.

The government of the United States is of the latter description. The powers of the legislature are defined and limited; and that those limits may not be mistaken or forgotten, the constitution is written. To what purpose are powers limited, and to what purpose is that limitation committed to writing; if these limits may, at any time, be passed by those intended to be restrained? The distinction between a government with limited and unlimited powers is abolished, if those limits do not confine the persons on whom they are imposed, and if acts prohibited [U.S. 137, 177] and acts allowed are of equal obligation. It is a proposition too plain to be contested, that the constitution controls any legislative act repugnant to it; or, that the legislature may alter the constitution by an ordinary act.

Between these alternatives there is no middle ground. The constitution is either a superior, paramount law, unchangeable by ordinary means, or it is on a level with ordinary legislative acts, and like other acts, is alterable when the legislature shall please to alter it.

If the former part of the alternative be true, then a legislative act contrary to the constitution is not law: if the latter part be true, then written constitutions are absurd attempts, on the part of the people, to limit a power in its own nature illimitable....

If an act of the legislature, repugnant to the constitution, is void, does it, notwithstanding its invalidity, bind the courts and oblige them to give it effect? Or, in other words, though it be not law, does it constitute a rule as operative as if it was a law? This would be to overthrow in fact what was established in theory; and would seem, at first view, an absurdity too gross to be insisted on. It shall, however, receive a more attentive consideration....

Those then who controvert the principle that the constitution is to be considered, in court, as a paramount law, are reduced to the necessity of maintaining that courts must close their eyes on the constitution, and see only the law.

This doctrine would subvert the very foundation of all written constitutions. It would declare that an act, which, according to the principles and theory of our government, is entirely void, is yet, in practice, completely obligatory. It would declare, that if the legislature shall do what is expressly forbidden, such act, notwithstanding the express prohibition, is in reality effectual. It would be giving to the legislature a practical and real omnipotence with the same breath which professes to restrict their powers within narrow limits. It is prescribing limits, and declaring that those limits may be passed at pleasure.

It is declared that "no tax or duty shall be laid on articles exported from any state." Suppose a duty on the export of cotton, of tobacco, or of flour; and a suit instituted to recover it. Ought judgment to be rendered in such a case? Ought the judges to close their eyes on the constitution, and only see the law?

The constitution declares that "no bill of attainder or ex post facto law shall be passed." If, however, such a bill should be passed and a person should be prosecuted under it, must the court condemn to death those victims whom the constitution endeavors to preserve?

"No person," says the constitution, "shall be convicted of treason unless on the testimony of two witnesses to the same overt act, or on confession in open court." Here the language of the constitution is addressed especially to the courts. It prescribes, directly for them, a rule of evidence not to be departed from. If the legislature should change that rule, and declare one witness, or a confession out of court, sufficient for conviction, must the constitutional principle yield to the legislative act?

From these and many other selections which might be made, it is apparent, that the framers of the constitution [5 U.S. 137, 180] contemplated that instrument as a rule for the government of courts, as well as of the legislature.

Why otherwise does it direct the judges to take an oath to support it? This oath certainly applies, in an especial manner, to their conduct in their official character. How immoral to impose it on them, if they were to be used as the instruments, and the knowing instruments, for violating what they swear to support!... Why does a judge swear to discharge his duties agreeably to the constitution of the United States, if that constitution forms no rule for his government? If it is closed upon him and cannot be inspected by him? If such be the real state of things, this is worse than solemn mockery. To prescribe, or to take this oath, becomes equally a crime.

It is also not entirely unworthy of observation, that in declaring what shall be the supreme law of the land, the constitution itself is first mentioned; and not the laws of the United States generally, but those only which shall be made in pursuance of the constitution, have that rank.

Thus, the particular phraseology of the constitution of the United States confirms and strengthens the principle, supposed to be essential to all written constitutions, that a law repugnant to the constitution is void, and that courts, as well as other departments, are bound by that instrument.

Too often, too many don't see the loss of freedom as that big of a deal. That's the way the people who steal freedom want it. They want the average citizen still at the job, worried about what he is going to put in his mouth more than what he can say with it. — Jefferson Mack, *Secret Freedom Fighter*

6. Stay out of the Deadbeat Dads Database

I am not anyone's father. I'm not even anyone's mother. I devoutly hope the government thinks I'm a muthah to deal with. But that's a different subject.

The fact is if I were to go get a job, any job, anywhere in the U.S., personal information about me would go into the federal Deadbeat Dads Database. It's not really the Deadbeat Dads Database. That's just the ploy that was used to sell it to the public. Here's how that worked: Back in 1996, those wild, radical Republican Revolutionaries wanted to keep government firmly *on* our backs while still pretending to get that clawing government monkey off. So they claimed it was a database to track parents who didn't pay child support. That made conservatives very happy, because they thought it meant cutting welfare spending. That made liberals very happy because, by golly, they were going to make those nasty old *men* pay their due.

But actually, the database has no connection — zero, zip, nada — to child-support judgments or parenthood. As soon as the database was established, as part of their alleged welfare reform law (Public Law 104-193), Congress and the media started admitting it was really a "New Hires Database." Well, that's not quite it, either. Because the law requires employers to inform on their employees every three months, you may be put into that database even if you've been working for a company for 25 years and are about to retire.

What it really is, is a Let's-Spy-on-*All*-Employed-Americans Database. A universal citizen-tracking scheme, slipped into law under cover of a Big Lie. And the Social Security number the political forebears of Mssrs. Clinton and Gingrich tricked your grandparents into accepting all those years ago is the code that makes it all possible. It is the "Open Sesame" that gives access to this, and many other, databases. This deadbeat politicians database is the most comprehensive citizen-tracking system ever devised by any government, anywhere.

Now, your mission, should you choose to accept it, is to *stay out of the damn thing*! Or, if you can't stay out of it, to screw it up so badly it's not useful to anybody. Here are some thoughts on how someone could do that. Some are just theory, mind you:

1. Be self-employed. We independent sorts are apparently not considered deadbeats, yet. And even when they do decide we're deadbeats... well... we're harder to catch.

2. Lie. If you have to be in the database, and your employer gives you a form to fill out, or lets you enter the data online, be sure you misspell everything, give wrong numbers, etc. Hope your employer doesn't "correct" it for you. Or hope the data-entry serf doing the "correcting" introduces other mistakes. Hooray for ineptitude!

3. Tell the truth, but in a way that confuses them. Cyndee Parker of Georgia's Coalition to Repeal the Fingerprints Law tells of a friend whose employer required him to fill out an unusually snoopy state version of the deadbeat dad's form. He truthfully answered that his spouse's

nickname was "Sweetheart" and that his personal physician was Jesus Christ.

4. Cultivate friends in the information services departments of your employer and various government agencies. Get them to screw up the data for you, to whatever extent they can.

5. Become a world-renowned computer cracker and destroy the system. Or make friends with someone of that sort.

6. Sue on Fourth Amendment grounds. Or Fifth Amendment grounds. You'll be correct. You'll lose, anyway, but some people just feel better trying to get justice through the courts.

7. Smash the computers. Naw, just kidding. Computers Are Our Friends.

8. Smash the people who want to track every moment of your life. Now there's an idea...

"There are three things that are always true when registries are created: One, there will always be more information collected than is needed to complete the task; two, it will always be kept longer than we are told; and, three, it will always be used for purposes other than intended." — Agneta Breitenstein, director of the Health Law Institute in Boston, as quoted in *Tracking Your Children Down,* by the Coalition for Constitutional Liberties

7. Databases and your children's health

The infamous Hillarycare fiasco of 1993 would — had it not been beaten back — have nationalized the entire U.S.

health-care system. One of its specifics was establishment of a federal database to track your child's immunization record from birth. Of course, a database that can track your child's immunization record can also be expanded to track anything else — beginning with other health records, then on to, say, psychological test results, family profiles, "fitness" for the workforce, suspicions about parents' political activities or politically incorrect habits and a host of other things that preoccupy bureaucrats.

But why worry? Hillarycare went down in flames as it resoundingly deserved to. Your children are safe from fed-snoops everywhere. And if you believe that...

No, Congress has been gradually implementing Hillarycare or something very much like it, ever since. In 1996, they planted several legal land mines in what they claimed was a "moderate" health care law. One of these secret provisions simply opened a back door into their original plan for your children. In the Health Insurance Portability and Accountability Act[2] they set up a fat bribe to the states and an authorization for the *states*, not the forbidden federal government, to collect and track immunization data on your child. Then Donna Shalala, the beloved Secretary of Health and Human Services, ordered the Social Security Administration to turn children's Universal Citizen ID (aka Social Security) numbers over to any state requesting them. *Your* permission is not required, mind you. The states are now merrily databasing away, using that good old "not for identification" number you were naïve enough to give your child.

Oh, and about that federal database that We the People said was a no-no? The Centers for Disease Control are al-

---

[2] Public Law 104-191, H.R. 3103, which became law on August 21, 1996, also known as the Kennedy-Kassebaum bill.

ready establishing a nice, helpful "National Immunization Registry Clearinghouse" (www.cdc.gov/nip/registry/). It's not a federal database, mind you. They wouldn't do *that* without the authorization of Congress, and against the stated will of The People, would they? Of course not! It's just to help coordinate state databases and make sure the states can all share information with each other. That's all. Totally benign. Yeah...

Until now, I've been neutral on the question of vaccinations. Most of us had 'em when we were kids and they didn't kill us. But on the other hand, when something becomes as much a part of a political agenda as children's immunizations have...well, you just have to wonder.

Some of us, of course, won't mind. There *is* a public health issue here. And most of us are going to be supremely disinclined to make a fuss over it. If you do decide to resist, or if you want to know more of the ins and outs of this issue, here are some things to think about.

If you have your children vaccinated, you might be tempted to try to have it done under false names, and certainly without using the Little Comrades' official government ID numbers. However, you must beware of the consequences of that attempt to keep your (and their) privacy. You already know your child probably won't be allowed into government school without a vaccination record, properly maintained under her little Universal ID. Well, government school's a bad place for the children of free people, anyway. But the Coalition for Constitutional Liberties (CCL) also reports that children are being denied health insurance and in some cases even being seized by the state on grounds of "child endangerment," merely because they weren't vaccinated. However, children who do go into the database can expect a lifetime of being tracked like cattle, and which is worse?

Keep in mind we ain't just talkin' measles and mumps here. The government now requires that little children all get vaccinated for hepatitis B, which is primarily a sexually transmitted disease![3]

According to the CCL, some states are already giving the little kiddies' names, addresses and Social Security numbers to any stranger who asks for them. (It probably helps if you pretend to be the kid's parent, though. Makes the bureaucrats pretend they're not breaching everyone's trust.) So you can expect information about your family to be shared with heaven knows what sort of people. Perhaps even worse people than bureaucrats!

And let's not forget that the same "accountability" act that created the children's database also set the stage for federal "standards" for the electronic transmission of *all* health care data — and once again, it'll be under your "unique identifier."

---

[3] Hepatitis B is indeed a horrible disease, and it is transmitted, like AIDS, via body-fluid-to-body-fluid contact. Preventive measures for those most at risk are no doubt an excellent idea. At-risk individuals include medical professionals, emergency workers, those with risky sexual practices, and intravenous drug users. However, a look at the stats may indicate that, once again, government is exacerbating a problem by overreacting, then using brute force to impose a solution. The number of hepatitis B cases in the U.S. has been steadily declining for years. According to the Centers for Disease Control's own figures, there were 18,003 cases in 1991, and fewer each year until, by 1997, there were only 8,749 in the country. On the other hand, as many as 17 percent of all those being vaccinated for hepatitis B may have adverse reactions; one-half- to one percent may have severe reactions, which include rheumatoid arthritis, brain damage or death. Vaccinate 50 million children and you've just condemned 250,000 to 500,000 of them to severe health problems, possibly fatal ones. All that to prevent fewer than 9,000 cases of a "politically trendy" disease???

"There are three things that are always true when registries are created…"

"So he [Thomas Pynchon] wants a private life and no photographs and nobody to know his home address. I can dig it; I can relate to that." — Salman Rushdie

8. Microsoft Anonymous: The 12 steps

A terrible addiction grips the world. It invades the most respectable middle-class homes and offices. It causes untold havoc. Yet, in this era when enlightened people understand that even coffee drinking ("caffeine use disorder") can be a serious disability, this addition goes unrecognized and untreated.

I speak of Microsoft addiction.

What is Microsoft addiction? It is hopeless dependence on a computer operating system that is more insecure than a junkie in a room full of narcs and more expensive than a hit of heroin. In the end, this addiction strips its users of all privacy and independence. This operating system is controlled by a ruthless multinational software cartel. Once you're caught in their .net like a drowning dolphin, Microsoft pushers know they can hook you on even more expensive software. Soon, you're mainlining the hard stuff… stuff like the infamous M$ Office XP — a program that not only costs more than XTC or cocaine, but reports your activities to your pusher, and demands that you get permission to "reactivate" the software simply because you dare to make changes in your system.

The M$ message: We own your computer. We own you. And your little dog, too.

Until now, the future has looked bleak for the ordinary victim hooked on Microsoft. But today, thousands are breaking free — and so can you! — thanks to the 12-step program of Microsoft Anonymous.

The 12 Steps to Microsoft Recovery

1. We admitted we were powerless over Microsoft — that our privacy had become negligible.

Microsoft's licensing agreements let the software cartel bust into your computer at any time. Microsoft lets its friends in, too. Privacy groups have found hidden keys within Windows — including one which *may* be for the exclusive use of the National Security Agency (NSA).

What Bill Gates doesn't do to you, some cracker will. There are more holes in Microsoft software than in a heroin addict's clammy gray flesh. Worms and viruses ooze through them like HIV through a dirty needle.

2. We came to believe that a different operating system could restore our sanity.

Linux (especially the easy-to-install Mandrake (www.linux-mandrake.com) or Red Hat (www.redhat.com/) can lift even the most hopeless Microsoft-head into a world of privacy and stability — and do it right on the same PC that now shares your Microsoft habit with you.

3. We made a decision to turn our computer systems over to Tux the Linux penguin as we understood him.

At first, we considered learning Urdu in order to read some of the manuals, but then decided to trust our instincts and that friendly Linux penguin.

Graphical "desktops" like KDE (www.kde.org/) and Gnome (www.gnome.org/), which come with Linux, comforted us with familiar point, drag-and-drop, pop-up menus, and other things to help us on our road to recovery. They even gave us "Redmond-style" graphical themes, helping us break Windows habit like Antabuse helps a wavering alcoholic.

4. We made a searching and fearless inventory of our applications and data files.

We understood that recovering from our Microsoft addiction might mean reformatting some of our data, surrendering familiar programs, and finding Linux equivalents. Fortunately, many distributions (brands) of Linux come with full office suites, Web browsers, e-mail programs, and everything we needed to get us going — all at no extra cost. Even the most vital applications of all — games.

Many Linux applications, like StarOffice, can convert and share data freely with their M$ equivalents. (Bill Gates, watch us break your hold even while those with whom we share data remain hooked!)

5. We admitted to tech support, to ourselves, and to another Linux newbie the exact nature of our misgivings.

Before buying, we visited Linux Newbie.org (www.linuxnewbie.org/) and LinuxChix.org (www.linuxchix.org/). We asked questions on their listservs about the Linux distributions other newcomers have tried and the pitfalls they'd encountered. Others in Microsoft recovery gave generously of their time and advice.

We asked experienced Linux gurus, too. But they mostly said things like "grep" and "tar -xvjf." We feared that "bunzip2" might be something dangerously kinky. We turned away when they asked about our boot sector partitions. (Some people just don't know when they're undermining the recovery process).

6. We were entirely ready to have Linux remove all those cookies, GUIDs, and trojan horses from our systems.

We prepared carefully for our first installation, had a good backup of our existing Windows system, and made sure that all our hardware was Linux compatible. We accepted that it wasn't always going to be easy, but that in the end it was going to free us from Microserfdom.

7. We humbly installed the operating system.

It turned out to be easier than we thought. Many Linux distributors now beckon weary Windows users with easy installation wizards and automatic hardware recognition — the very temptations that first drove many of us into the clutches of Microsoft.

8. We made a list of all the software we used and became willing to use alternatives.

Some of us decided we needed a dual-boot system, with both Linux and Windows on it, because critical software was available only under Windows. But we resisted remaining Windows dependent.

We used Linux for a task any time we possibly could. The more we used Linux, the easier it became. The more we used Windows... well, when you find yourself insisting, "I can turn off Windows any time I want. Really I can"... you should be worried. Be very, very worried.

9. We downloaded alternative software where possible, but never a Microsoft product.

Linux isn't just for techies any more. But now that IBM, Hewlett-Packard, the NSA, and yes, even Microsoft, are getting on the Linux wagon, beware. We continue to avoid products from companies with a history of snooping into our computers and our e-mail.

10. We continued to take personal inventory and when we were leaving security holes, promptly repaired them.

Linux, being open source, can be examined by any software engineer to make sure it has no hidden security holes — unlike Microsoft, whose owners hide its code like Columbian drug traffickers hide their profits in Cayman Island banks.

Linux is harder for crackers to target. And if you're worried about another sort of cracker — the government or corporate kind — think about this. Those "key loggers" or keystroke monitoring programs? Virtually every one of them works only with Windows — and against Windows users.

Still, we diligently research before installing upgrades, and we regularly read electronic privacy e-mail alerts.

11. We sought through user groups, books, whitepapers, and HOWTOS to improve our conscious knowledge of Linux, searching only for understanding and the power to improve data security, system stability, and personal freedom.

We told ourselves, "Even if the manual is written in an obscure French-Ecuadorian dialect of Swahili, it's worth the effort."

Increasingly, Web sites, books, and manuals for new users led us along our way. Listservs dedicated to our chosen distributions offered answers to our questions. We persevered, helped by those who'd gone before.

12. Having had a computational awakening as the result of these steps, we tried to carry this message to Window users and to practice these principles in all our affairs.

And that's what we're doing right now.

Sometimes, you have to hit bottom before you're ready for recovery. Remember us the next time your screen turns that funny blue color, and pressing CTRL-ALT-DEL for an hour only gives you blisters on your fingers. Remember us next time your data ends up in an FBI dossier. Remember us next time some 13-year-old called H@ckWit infects your Microsoft Outlook with a virus that converts your hard drive into strawberry Jell-o.

You will be among friends at Microsoft Anonymous.

NOTE: I wrote "MIcrosoft Anonymous" with Debra Ricketts and a little help from Charles Curley. It first appeared in the members-only section of SierraTimes.com. This version has been edited especially for this book.

9. Listen up, you state governments!!!

Because I could not possibly say it better, I quote extensively from Gene Sharp's superb trilogy, *The Politics of Nonviolent Action*, specifically from book two, *The Methods of Nonviolent Action:*[4]

> One of the early and crucial constitutional problems of the United States government after its establishment was the question of who would determine when a law or action had exceeded or violate[d] the purposes and powers set out by the new Constitution. Although the Supreme Court soon assumed this role, this was not the only possibility. Thomas Jefferson and James Madison developed the doctrine of nullification, which said that the legislature of a given state could decide that an Act passed by Congress violated the Constitution, and hence was null and void within that state. This was the basis for the famous Virginia Resolutions of 1798 and the Kentucky Resolutions of 1798 and 1799.
>
> Aroused by the antidemocratic tendencies in the new United States government, of which he saw the Alien and

---

[4] *The Politics of Non-Violent Action, Part Two, The Methods of Nonviolent Action*, by Gene Sharp, Extending Horizons Books, Boston, 1973.

Sedition Acts as only the beginning, Thomas Jefferson concluded that it was necessary to erect a strong barrier against the encroachments of the Federal Government. He privately participated in drafting these resolutions, introduced in both Kentucky and Virginia. (James Madison introduced them in the Virginia Assembly.) One of the 1798 Kentucky Resolutions declared:

> *Resolved*, that the several States composing the United States of America, are not united on the principle of unlimited submission to their general government; but that...they constituted a general government for special purposes...; and that whensoever the general government assumes undelegated powers, its acts are unauthoritative, void, and of no force.

It further asserted that the constituent states, not the federal government itself, must be able to judge when the Constitution had been exceeded.

One of the Virginia Resolutions of that year also asserted that when the Federal Government had exceeded its constitutionally authorized powers, "the states, who are parties thereto, have the right and are in duty bound to interpose for arresting the progress of the evil, and for maintaining within their respective limits the authorities, rights, and liberties appertaining to them." The 1799 Kentucky Resolutions asserted that extension of the activities of the Federal Government beyond the bounds set by the Constitution would lead to "an annihilation of the state governments...," and that the doctrine that the Federal Government alone should judge the extent of its constitutionally delegated powers, not the constituent states, would lead to a process of increasing federal powers which would "stop not short of *despotism*..."

This theory was the basis for the nullification doctrine adopted by Vice-President John C. Calhoun in 1828, when he denounced the tariff law of that year. Calhoun claimed the right of a state to declare inoperative within its boundaries any law that it judged to be unconstitutional. He saw this as an alternative to secession and as a defense of the

Constitution. This general doctrine was later extended by certain states to actual secession from the Union. By itself secession was not an act of war; it only became so when military clashes occurred between Union troops and secessionist soldiers. (Had slavery — an institution impossible to defend by nonviolent means — not existed in the South and had the South wished to secede on other grounds, it is theoretically possible that it might have done so and applied a widespread program of nonviolent noncooperation which would have been, given a very different type of society in the South, very difficult indeed for Federal forces to crush.)

Now, I am under no illusion that state governments are, or ever would be, any sort of noble defenders of liberty. They're just governments and all they want is whatever amount of power we people will let them seize. Furthermore I'm a constitutionalist only to the extent of taking the position, "The Constitution isn't perfect, but it's better than what we have now."[5]

Nevertheless, listen to the above and imagine what a different course this country might take if some of our cowardly, sell-out state governments stopped trading their citizens' freedom for federal bribes (bribes with their own residents' stolen money!) and stood up to the fedgov.

Vermont? Colorado? Wyoming? Idaho? Arizona? Nevada? Montana? Kentucky? Tennessee? Are you listening? Forget those namby-pamby no-teeth "Tenth Amendment Resolutions" some of you have been primly passing. Declaring that states actually *do* have guaranteed rights, as you have been doing with these resolutions, is silly. Of course, states have rights! Period. Do something that takes real courage, for a change. Your ancestor governments created this

---

[5] For an enlightening view of the Constitution, read *Hologram of Liberty*, by Ken Royce (Boston T. Party), Javelin Press, 1998.

fedmonster as a beast of burden to serve a union of independent states. Put the monster back in its cage! We ordinary people are doing the best we can, but we're having a hard time doing it while you sell our rights to the feddies. Even if all you're interested in is turf and not our rights, stand up and fight, for heaven's sake!

The impunity and indifference with which our constitutional protections have been trashed can lead to only two logical conclusions: (a) Those who have been elected to represent We the People have knowingly committed high crimes against the true sovereign. As such, immediate removal would be the most genteel of punishments. (b) Those who have been elected to represent We the People have UNknowingly committed high crimes against the true sovereign. As such, immediate removal would be the most genteel of punishments. — Wayne Dennis Holt

10. Why should they stop when nobody punishes them?

With every federal outrage that blats across the media I become more convinced of one thing: Government agencies will never stop being abusive, because no one forces them to stop. Few individual agents are ever held accountable for their actions. There is no price to pay for doing evil.

Theoretically, the justice system is there to make sure wrongdoers are punished and to deter others from thinking they can get away with the same crimes. In reality, the "justice" system generally protects the Lords of Government and crushes those who fight them.

Little goatherder Ezequiel Hernandez bleeds to death in the Texas wasteland while his killers, U.S. Marines, stand around watching. No charges are ever brought against them. The butchers of Waco walk free, while the survivors of Waco languish in hellish prisons. Vicki, Sammy and Striker Weaver lie dead, while Lon Horiuchi enjoys his independence and Larry Cooper gets an award for shooting Sammy in the back. A federal judge, in dismissing charges against Horiuchi, even declared that *no* federal employee performing his duties has to obey *any* state law. Ever. Think about that next time you're facing a fed.

Yes, in the Weaver and Hernandez cases, "the government" paid millions in reparations. But who felt any personal sting? Who received any lesson in humane conduct? Nobody. The individual do-ers, and those who want to emulate them, learned the opposite — that they are free to harm anyone they wish, as long as they're on duty. Why should they stop? What possible motivation is there for government agents to behave in any other way than horribly? Congress won't stop them. The courts won't. We must, or we will be crushed like bugs. The only obstacle now is finding the appropriate way to halt their depredations. It's not an easy problem, but it's one all freedom lovers should be working to solve.

We are fast approaching the stage of the ultimate inversion: the stage where the government is free to do anything it pleases, while the citizens may act only by permission; which is the stage of the darkest periods of human history, the stage of rule by brute force. — Ayn Rand, *"The Nature of Government"*

---

11. Take the frog-boiling challenge

We have all heard that if you put a frog into boiling water, it will immediately leap out, whereas if you put froggie into cold water and gradually heat the pot, the critter will stay put until it dies. Froggie, of course, is us. The water is tyranny. And the hand turning up the heat belongs to the tyrants.

The following questionnaire assesses your opinions on the frog's condition, and was inspired by an Internet note from Dennis Justice.

1. Current condition of the frog

a) Nice and cool

b) Comfortably warm

c) Getting a little hot in here, but handleable

d) Hm. Getting awfully hot. Starting to burn froggie's little footies

e) Hey, this hurts like hell! Will the people who are running things please come and turn the heat down?

f) Hey, maybe froggie ought to think about jumping out, but...well, that's a lot of trouble. He might land on a hot burner and get hurt. Let's wait and see what happens

g) Ouch! Ouch! Ouch! Anybody with any sense would jump out — THIS MINUTE!

h) Too late. Froggie passes out

i) Froggie cooked.

2. When should froggie jump?

a) Froggie shouldn't have gotten into anybody's damn pot, anyway

b) He should jump when it's still nice and cool

c) When it's comfortably warm

d) When it starts getting a little hot, but handleable

e) When it starts to burn froggie's little footies

f) When it gets to the point where it could do some serious damage

g) When it's a choice between jumping and death

h) Never. The people who put froggie in the pot obviously know what's best for him.

3. At what point will YOU jump?

a) I'm not in the pot. Everything's fine

b) I'll jump when it's still nice and cool

c) I'll jump when it's comfortably warm

d) I'll jump when it starts getting a little hot, but handleable

e) I'll jump when it starts to burn my feet

f) I'll jump when it gets to the point where it could do some serious damage

g) I'll jump when it's a choice between jumping and death

h) Never. The people who put me in the pot obviously know what's best for me.

Bonus questions for extra credit:

4. Why hasn't froggie jumped yet?

5. What should froggie do if the whole kitchen is full of guys in black ninja suits?

6. **What, if anything, would a smart froggie do to or about those who'd put him in the pot?**

Answers: There are no "right" answers. This is just something to think about.

> *Our government has kept us in a perpetual state of
> fear — kept us in a continuous stampede of patriotic
> fervor — with the cry of grave national emergency...
> Always there has been some terrible evil to gobble us
> up if we did not blindly rally behind it by furnishing the
> exorbitant sums demanded. Yet, in retrospect, these
> disasters seem never to have happened, seem never to
> have been quite real.* — General Douglas MacArthur,
> 1957

12. How things have changed

This item isn't a to-do, but a personal observation necessi-
tated by a revision and update to this book.

I wrote *Don't Shoot the Bastards (Yet)* in the fall of 1998. I
revised it in 2002. Much of what you see as you hold this
book in your hands is exactly what I wrote originally, with
updated addresses and URLs. But how much has changed!

In 1998, we were poised on the edge of the abyss-that-
wasn't, Y2K. Since then, we've collapsed into the abyss that
so tragically was and is.

First, the election of George W. Bush made many 1990s
freedom activists complacent. After eight years of Clinton
bashing, a lot of people relaxed. Even if they didn't exactly
believe all would be well, they were tired, relieved, and
ready to let their guard down.

Then came September 11, 2001, anthrax mailings, airline
shoe bombers, a war in the east, and a much larger (and perhaps endless) War Against Terrorism. For a time, we all be-

came patriots and rallied 'round — while a "conservative" government, in the name of "preserving freedom," imposed upon us Draconian police-state measures most of us would never have tolerated from Clinton, and never tolerated from anyone before September 11.

The very government that failed to protect us against a long-planned suicide bombing cried, "Trust us, trust us" — and a shaken public, against all logic, did exactly that, to our own detriment.

As events reel out behind us into history, we reel ahead into lord knows what frightening, constricted, heavily surveilled future.

Yet the freedom movement remains quieter now than it was in 1998. As I look back on what I wrote then, one constant theme was that of confrontations, sieges, preparation, organized resistance to authority — and an increasing tendency on the part of authority to see certain American citizens (particularly patriots, constitutionalists, militia members, and the like) as the enemy.

This was the mood of the 1990s. It is no more. Many of the organized resistance groups are gone. Law enforcement has become more careful about laying fatal sieges. And — for the moment, at least — many former advocates of freedom are still cheering for the federal government's new wiretapping, bank surveillance, inter-agency information sharing, warrantless searches, and indefinite detention powers, under the naïve belief that these horrors will only affect "foreign terrorists."

In the meantime, not a single one of the dozens and dozens of rights we've lost since 1913 or 1933 or 1934 or 1968 has been restored to us. Nobody — including we ourselves (so conditioned to losing) expected anything different. Government takes power and rights. Only under the harshest pressure or threat of rebellion does it ever give them back.

So as I sat down to revise this book, I was faced with a country that has become less free, yet (ironically) also faced with a freedom movement that cares less and is less spirited in resistance, and I was faced with trying to make this book fit that reality.

I've entirely replaced several items that had clearly become obsolete or that feet hopelessly "quaint" in the present climate. At the same time, I've left in others (like items 26, 31, 54, 76, 97, and 101) that don't fit the mood of the moment, but that I believe may — should — will — fit a future day.

The main thing to remember is that, while government agencies aren't currently focusing as intently on painting certain Americans as the enemy, the totality of government policy now presumes that *every* American — and everyone else — is a criminal suspect. That, after all, is the rationale behind airport body searches, streetside surveillance cameras, random checkpoints, monitoring of ordinary financial transactions, and so on. Police and bureaucrats are waiting for each and every one of us to commit a crime so they can clamp down on us.

Government policy is more dangerous now than it was just a few years ago. There are many reasons I can state that, but one reason is that these types of random investigation aren't the best ways to catch serious criminals or terrorists, but they are among the best ways to harass, intimidate, incriminate, and ultimately infuriate ordinary citizens.

Ultimately, I do believe more and more ordinary citizens will become infuriated. And I believe the freedom movement will rise again. So if a few things in this book don't seem contemporary, look at them again in five years, or 10.

> *The government consists of a gang of men exactly*
> *like you and me. They have, taking one with another,*
> *no special talent for the business of government; they*
> *have only a talent for getting and holding office. Their*
> *principal device to that end is to search out groups*
> *who pant and pine for something they can't get and to*
> *promise to give it to them. Nine times out of ten that*
> *promise is worth nothing. The tenth time is made good*
> *by looting A to satisfy B. In other words, government is*
> *a broker in pillage, and every election is sort of an ad-*
> *vance auction sale of stolen goods.* — H. L. Mencken

13. Don't join lobbying groups

It's very easy for us to send a donation or join a group and feel as if we're doing something for the cause of liberty. Sometimes we are. Sometimes all we're doing is desperately trying to make ourselves feel better. Sometimes we're actually combating freedom.

Take groups that lobby Congress. (Please!) What do they do? Take your money, go to the people who are rampaging over your rights, and ask them politely if they'd consider treading a little more softly. Sometimes these groups are even "successful." But success, by these standards, usually means getting one or two onerous, illegal provisions removed from a bill that has dozens of them and should never become law at all. Even more often, it means getting a provision "softened." Softened! Isn't that just what we need? Softer abuse, softer injustice, softer unconstitutionality.

These groups and their supporters will point out how much worse things would be without their efforts. That *may* be true in the very short run. But how much worse do things get in the long run because they help make the march of tyranny less obvious and therefore more palatable? This is just a way to turn up the water under the pot a little more slowly. Is that what you want? We don't need to *slow* tyranny. We don't need to be grateful that the jackboot is only grinding our chest and not our face.

No, the only thing that helps us is living free and — if we have the numbers or the will — putting tyrants on notice that America belongs to the people, not to anyone who has the power to spew out a law.

If you feel you must send someone 25 bucks or 500 bucks in hopes they might slow tyranny through lobbying, that's very understandable. There are a few groups, like Gun Owners of America, that are utterly sincere and uncompromising in what they attempt to accomplish. But their power is limited, and if you send them money you must realize you haven't actually *done something* for freedom. You've just *asked them* to do what they can. Spend your hard-earned bucks on direct and effective action for freedom. If you must send bucks to groups, don't let yourself stop there. Go out and seize a bit of freedom back from the liberty thieves. Do it directly. Do it yourself. Do it *for* yourself and for the future.

"Barbara Mostel... was waiting for a bus on Avenue of the Americas a few hours after the Rockefeller Center Christmas tree lighting in 1996 when cops on horseback and on foot began yelling at her to move.

"Eventually, she says, one of them moved her, picking her up and throwing her down on the pavement. Her arm, back, and head were injured.

"'I should be grateful. I'm a small woman, 93 pounds and 5 feet 4 inches,' she said the other day. 'I guess if I were a big man, [the police officer would] have shot me.'

"Ms. Mostel said the officer gave her his badge and precinct numbers when asked, but they weren't his real ones. An artist, she drew pictures of him for the Civilian Complaint Review Board, but [police] officers claimed to be unable to find him.

Her lawyer is Joel Berger and — Lipsyte reports — "Berger found most poignant her vain attempt to get other officers on the scene to be witnesses for her." — Robert Lipsyte, New York *Times*, March 29, 1998 (as quoted by columnist Nat Hentoff, April 28, 1998)

14. "Bad cop! No donut!"

As the book title so vividly makes clear, "The Policeman is [NOT] Your Friend."[7] It might be nice to have cops around if someone steals your car, or if you're being held hostage by a crazed control freak with a gun. But we need to keep their usefulness in perspective.

These days, the policeman is likely to *be* the guy stealing your car or breaking down your door in a screaming rage. The cop *is* the crazed control freak with the gun. But even

---

[7] *The Policeman is Your Friend and Other Lies* by Ned Beaumont, Loompanics Unlimited, 1996. For an informative view of your rights in the era of warrantless searches, random checkpoints and civil forfeiture, also see *You & the Police*, by Boston T. Party.

before cops across America became militarized, brutalized
and corrupted by federal money and private loot (yours),
their importance was exaggerated and their mentality not always friendly to freedom.

Did you know that this country, from the day of its first
European colonization, went 235 years without even having
a single professional police force? The first full-time, professional police force in the entire *world* wasn't formed until
1829, after thousands of years of civilization![8] If cops are so
vital, why did it take so long to invent them? Has "public
safety" improved since governments set a uniformed class of
professional enforcers onto our city streets?

Even among those police who have an honest commitment
to freedom, their first loyalties are nearly always to uniforms
and the people who wear them, not to principles. Here's an
example:

Jack McLamb, retired Phoenix policeman and founder of
Police Against the New World Order, went to the Shirley
Allen siege (see Item 54) to see what he could learn firsthand, and presumably to give his support to a lady whose
rights were being violated. The Illinois State cops — no
dummies — never let McLamb near Allen. Instead, they
took him aside, separated him from his traveling companion,
J.J. Johnson, and, for two hours, explained the situation entirely from their own point of view. They kept him behind
what is known as "the blue wall" — the police us-against-
them mentality that's fostered from police academy onward.

Armed with nothing but a second-hand, one-sided view
(but a view that came from brother officers) McLamb stood

---

[8]Sir Robert Peel invented the modern police force, in London, in 1829. New York
didn't have a professional police force until 1844. Both dates are according to en-
cyclopedia.com.

up before an audience at a rally and, to everyone's shock, announced that the cops were right and that he'd have shot Shirley Allen himself, if she'd pointed a gun at him (as she did when state police officers, in plain clothes, first tried to carry her off her property "for her own good"). McLamb apparently no longer retained any thought that, just perhaps, a completely innocent homeowner protecting herself against an unconstitutional, quasi-legal, invasion might have a right, or even a duty, to stand against the invaders. Now *that's* cop mentality.

I've met Jack McLamb. I know he's a kind, sincere, thoroughly decent person. This is not intended to single him out for a slap. It's just to show that even a cop who preaches the credo of freedom is a cop first, freedom lover second. And when being a cop conflicts with being a freedom lover, he's a cop all the way.

It's not my intention to bash every cop in the world, or even any specific cop I know. My local cops, for instance, appear to be pretty cool people. However, I will verbally bash every single one of them who enforces unjust laws or who practices an us-against-them mentality to the point of forgetting that we have rights — even and especially when we're dealing with *them.*

Sometimes they're good to have around. I just wouldn't recommend trusting one as far as I could drop kick 'em. And I *would* recommend keeping that in mind at all times when dealing with them — even when they're helping you retrieve your kid's lost tricycle or trying to figure out what rabid varmint beat and raped you. The policeman is not your friend.

*With Republicans in power, man exploits man. With
Democrats, just the opposite! — bumper sticker*

15. Don't waste time worrying about legislation

Total Waste of Time #376: Getting agitated about bills and
bad laws. Don't worry about what Congress or your state
legislature is about to do to you or has just done to you. It's a
waste of time. Really it is.

Yes, yes, this viewpoint goes against everything they
taught you in civics class. But I *know* it's a waste of time because I sometimes do it myself, and I speak with the voice of
experience.

The original *101 Things* grew out of my fury over a mon-
strosity of the 104th Congress called HR 666, a bill that, had
it passed both houses and been signed into law, would have
gutted what little is left of our Fourth Amendment protected
rights against illegal search and seizure. (It fortunately
passed only one house.) My other recent book, *I Am Not a
Number!* was a direct result of the passage of national ID
legislation (Public Law 104-208, and others) perpetrated by
that same Congress the following year. So how can I sit here
and say you shouldn't let the badness get to you when I let it
get to me to the point of writing books over it?

Well, it's because I've traveled a long road to reach important conclusions. To wit:

All laws now being passed are bad.

There were some good ones at one time, like laws to punish people for being violent to the innocent, but there's
nothing left now but the itchy little longings of compulsive
control freaks and special interests.

Even when a law is proposed with good intentions, it's still bad.

Realistically, no 100-percent-good bill will ever get through any legislative body. A bill may start as someone's earnest effort to "correct" earlier bad laws or court judgments or to undo some injustice. But even those rarities will either be so ill-conceived, or end up being so loaded with dreck before they're passed that the end result will be negative. And since almost no laws ever get repealed these days, the badness keeps compounding and compounding. Laws that try to undo it simply create more of the same chaos.

Your congressthing, remember, doesn't give a rat's butt about your opinion, unless you're rich, own a major corporation, or are one of three zillion people screaming at her about an issue.

My god, you don't actually believe you can *reason* with these creatures, do you? Even if he *could* do something to stop the ever-growing horrors oozing out of Washington, your congressbeing isn't *going* to. So don't waste your incredibly valuable time trying for the impossible. You have more productive things to do.

You're already an outlaw a thousand times over, anyway. So why worry about one more law that you and everybody else will inevitably break? So go ahead. Be aware. It's always good to know what they're going to do to you next. But just don't get in a frazzle and waste your time fighting a battle you can't win. In the great scheme of life, what's one more silly damned law, more or less? We're already living in a police state. From here on, it's just a matter of degree, not kind. Ho hum.

Let them pass their horrible laws, one by one. Let the mass of people experience for themselves the laws they once wished upon their neighbors, or the laws they didn't bother to learn about. Then let them be shocked. And then pissed.

Remember:

> **Law-spewers only imagine they have control**
> **of anything.**
> **Bad laws are made to be broken.**
> **Don't let such pathetic, maladjusted twits control**
> **your mind or your time.**

I would sooner live in a society governed by the first two thousand names in the Boston telephone directory than in a society governed by the two thousand faculty members of Harvard University. — William F. Buckley, Jr.

16. Things to do while fighting the urge to write to congresscritters

Okay, even when your head *knows* it's a waste of time, sometimes your fingers absolutely twitch to write letters to congresscritters. You've read the morning paper and learned about the latest piece of blithering idiocy some Glorious Leader is perpetrating, and you think you must, just one more time, try to talk some freedom into that *thing* out there in DC who imagines "more government" is the only answer to every question.

Stop! Breathe! You don't have to do it! Here are some other things you can do *right this minute* to combat that urge for one more letter! Right now, while your hands are shaking with that old unhealthy desire, do one of these things instead.

These, by the way, are all things you can do to brighten your own, personal life. In Item 36 we'll cover some things that you can do to help right wrongs in others' lives:

1. Go to a garage sale or junk store and find an old bike or other simple piece of machinery you can repair.

2. Put on your favorite CD, really, really *loud* and dance until you fall over.

3. Order some storage foods, or make a trip to the grocery store and buy a few items to put away for hard times.

4. Look around the room you're in and ask how ready it is for a siege or disaster. Then do something to make it more ready.

5. Store a cache of camping goods somewhere and practice getting to it quickly and using it without needing to add a lot of other things.

6. Read, and carefully study, at least one book on self-defense or self-sufficiency. Then practice one or more of its techniques.

7. Set a target for learning some new skill and work until you've reached it.

8. Go to the shooting range and spend an hour potting targets.

9. Take a walk in the nearest park, forest or open field and remind yourself that *this* is what life is about, not politics.

10. Build a stone wall or brick patio. Work in your garden. Anything that involves handling earthy materials can have an almost magical effect on your perception of what's important in life.

11. Play with your children or grandchildren. Or your dogs.

12. Get puking drunk. Shoot heroin. Dash in front of a runaway semi. *Anything* is more productive and more sensible than giving in to that trembling urge to write to a congressthing!

> *Madam Speaker, while everybody in Washington is talking about a fly on our face, an elephant may be eating our assets.* — James Traficant, D-Ohio, February 5, 1998

17. History of the income tax (No, not *this* income tax)

Did you know that the United States got its first income tax in 1862 — and that Congress actually repealed the beastie? The history of that tax is quite instructive. An acquaintance was kind enough to send photocopied pages from *An American Almanac of 1878*,[9] from which I excerpted the following passages. (Emphasis in the text is mine.) Read 'em and weep:

THE HISTORY OF THE INCOME TAX

The first income tax was passed by Congress July 1, 1862, and took effect in the year 1863. It taxed all incomes over $600 and under $10,000 at the rate of three per cent, and on all over $10,000 it levied a tax of five percent... By the act of March 3, 1865, the income tax law was amended so as to increase the three percent tax to five percent, and the five percent tax on incomes over $10,000 was changed

---

[9] *An American Almanac of 1878*, edited by Ainsworth R. Spofford, Librarian of Congress; published by The American News Company and manufactured by S.W. Green, 16 and 18 Jacob Street, New York City.

to a ten percent tax upon the excess over $5,000 income, the exemption of $600 remaining the same...

The income tax was further amended, March 2, 1867, so as to increase the exemption, then standing at $600, up to $1,000. At the same time all discrimination as to the taxing of large incomes [at] a higher rate was abolished and the tax was fixed at five per cent on all incomes in excess of $1,000. The act also contained the limitation or proviso that the taxes on incomes should be levied and collected until and including, the year 1870, and no longer...

The agitation against the income tax, which finally led to its repeal, was perhaps *far more owing to the excess of the rate charged* than to any real objection to the tax itself. Special Commissioner David A. Wells, in his report on the revenue system for the year 1869, set forth the fact that *an income tax of five percent was greater than had ever been imposed, by any other nation, except in time of war, or in extraordinary national exigencies.* He recommended the reduction of the tax from five percent to three percent on all incomes over $1,000, accompanying the suggestion with an expression of opinion that an assessment of three percent would probably yield to the Treasury a sum almost, if not quite equal to that collected at five percent. The reason assigned for this was, that while the reduction of the rate would afford a great and welcome relief to the classes then paying it, it would at the same time bring within reach of the income tax law great numbers who had hitherto avoided giving in their receipts at all, or had made imperfect or fraudulent returns, in order to escape the excessive tax. *"A tax of five percent," said Commissioner Wells, "is evidently too high for revenue purposes."*

In March 1871, Congress abolished the excessive and controversial income tax. And guess what? At its most intrusive and outrageous "...the tax was paid during 1868 by only 250,000 persons out of the entire population of almost

40,000,000..." What are we putting up with, people? And when do we say No?

> *When evil wins in the world, it is only by the default of the good. That is why one man of reason and moral stature is more important actually and potentially, than a million fools.* — Ayn Rand

18. Overcoming inertia

This is not the time for discussion, but for action. Too many of us in the freedom movement have psyched ourselves into belief systems in which all we can do is talk. On one extreme some of you, my fellow libertarians, are yammerheads who are going to be debating natural rights vs. chaos theory as the stormtroopers kick down your door. On the other extreme, some of you, my "right-wing conspiracist" friends, have got yourselves so freaked out by the belief that distant entities control the world that you act as if there's not a single, effective thing you can do to increase your freedom and the freedom of those around you. Well, philosophy is important, and if there is a conspiracy running the globe, we should learn about it, no doubt. But *talk ain't action.* No matter what else may be going on in the universe, we all can, and ought to be, taking steps to increase freedom in our own lives. Mental steps. Financial steps. Practical steps such as laying in food, water or medicines. Self-defense steps. Networking steps. Organizing steps. Whatever. But for pete's sake — ACT! SENSIBLY!!!!!

I thoroughly disapprove of duels. If a man should challenge me, I would take him kindly and forgivingly by the hand and lead him to a quiet place and kill him.
— Mark Twain

19. Most important freedom-fighting weapon to acquire
Brain: Equipped with right attitude.

The children who know how to think for themselves, spoil the harmony of the collective society that is coming, where everyone [would be] interdependent. — John Dewey, educational philosopher, 1899

20. Yes, I really meant that about your TV
Some readers complained vociferously about two items in *101 Things*: "Don't write your congresscritter" and "Kill your TV." They protested that writing to congressthings was some sort of inborn civic responsibility, even when it didn't do any good. Well, I won't argue with anyone's religion, however irrational. Those who feel compelled to write useless letters are as welcome to their rituals as those who once felt commanded to flagellate themselves bloody on medieval roadways to atone for their sins.

But the TV thing was more interesting. The argument there seemed to be, "Well, of course, I understand what you're saying, but I *need* to watch television so... um... so... ah... so I'll be aware of what's going on in the American cultural climate and in the media. Yeah, that's why I watch TV."

Well, it is true we need to know both our cultural surroundings and the techniques of our enemies (of which the mainstream media is certainly one). There are many ways to do that, from hanging out at your local bowling alley or garden club to reading a major metropolitan newspaper. But if you want to achieve cultural and media enlightenment through watching television, I suggest you'll get a *much* sharper picture if you turn off the tube *now*, then turn *on* the tube a year from now and make yourself sit through a single evening's programming, from local news to the late-late show. Now, *that* will give you a great big insight into the media culture.

On the other hand, when you immerse yourself in television every day you become such a part of it that you *can't* see it with any detachment. If you look at it after a year of sanity, you'll see a thousand things you never noticed while mentally swimming in the TV swamp.

I've been without a television since December 27, 1994. Since then, the only cultural deprivation I've suffered is this: I have no idea what Budweiser has to do with frogs. I don't know why everybody thinks a taco-peddling Chihuahua is so cute. Jerry Springer has never entered my living room. And I've never seen a purple dinosaur. Otherwise, I am *more* aware of my culture than I was before. And a happier human being, to boot.

For more information on the insidious effects of the TV media itself (not just its content), read *The Plug-In Drug* by Marie Winn and *Four Arguments for the Elimination of Television* by Jerry Mander, both available through Amazon.com.

Remember: When you watch TV, your brain is operating largely in delta and alpha wave mode. That means you are *hypnotized* and almost certainly not fully aware of all the subtle impressions you're receiving. The medium, not just the message, is pernicious for that reason. If you're telling yourself you have to sit and watch television by the hour in order to understand American culture or observe media influence, then I say you're in denial about why you're really sitting in front of that mind-control box and you're a prime and rather scary example of media influence in action. And think of what it's doing to your children! Get free. Kill your TV.

> *[The Chinese] are a kindly-disposed, well-meaning race, and are respected and well treated by the upper classes, all over the Pacific coast. No Californian gentleman or lady ever abuses or oppresses a Chinaman, under any circumstances, an explanation that seems to be much needed in the East. Only the scum of the population do it — they and their children; they, and, naturally and consistently, the policemen and politicians, likewise, for these are the dust-licking pimps and slaves of the scum, there as well as elsewhere in America.* — Mark Twain, *Roughing It,* 1871

21. All that ever needs to be said about racism

This year, several white supremacists have oozed into my life. One altered an article of mine to suit his own purposes, then circulated it with my byline still attached. Another claimed me and two other fine libertarian writers as his allies — until we declared loudly across the Internet that we abhorred both his desire for violence and his injustice to individuals. At that point, he pronounced — to our great relief and considerable amusement — that he'd actually known all along that we were cowardly dogs and unspeakable phonies, unfit to shine the shoes of his Nazi friends.

I support the right of even the most loathsome toad to believe his own beliefs. I emphatically support the right of all people to choose their own associates, employees and neighbors. If you don't want to associate with blue-eyed blonds, no one should have the right to force you to. Likewise blacks, Hispanics, Amway dealers, crazed feminists, fans of Britney Spears, conservative politicians, liberal do-gooders, or men who comb their hair over their bald spots. It's your taste, your life and your business whom you associate with.

That said, I just don't get racism. I certainly don't get why the media persists in considering all freedom lovers racists, or why a few racists do, in fact, cling to the freedom movement, when they want control over others, not freedom for all. I also don't get how politicians and allegedly liberal social reformers can openly advocate racism (i.e., affirmative apartheid) and not be damned for their desire to subjugate any portion of the population to any other.

But then I ran across the following on the Web site of science fiction writer and futurist, Robert Anton Wilson (http://www.rawilson.com). Reading it gave me an "aha!" — a brand new, yet undeniable insight about why racism is currently so prevalent in the world.

> When I was in high school and college... we all remembered Hitler very well. Teachers taught us that Hitler was terrible, not because he hated the wrong group, but because hating any group is illogical, unscientific and leads ultimately to violence. Groups are grammatical fictions; only individuals exist, and each individual is different.
>
> Sometime while I was busy and didn't notice, Political Correctness took over Academia and they stopped teaching that. They started teaching that Hitler was terrible because he hated the wrong group, but it's okay to hate other groups...

This rebellion against rationality originally intended to make Radical Feminism and its doctrine of male fungibility respectable, and it succeeded, at least in the major media, but it also made fungible group hatred respectable in general. Now the anti-Semites and all the other hate mongers are crawling out from under their rocks, and Academia does not have the ammunition to argue against them. Academia cannot argue the rational principle that hatred of any group does not make sense; they dumped that when they dumped logic (as a "male" perversion).

The argument between Left and Right now consists only of debating which are the correct groups to hate.

And there were always choices to make. Every day, every hour offered the opportunity to make a decision, a decision which determined whether you would or would not submit to those powers which threatened to rob you of your very self, your inner freedom... — Viktor Frankl, *Man's Search for Meaning* (on his experience in a Nazi concentration camp)

22. Join the Tyranny Response Team

The Tyranny Response Team, founded in Colorado by Bob Glass and an enthusiastic group of compatriots, has spread across the country and put thousands of opponents into a tizzy.

TRT is non violent, but is confrontational, and in-your face — a "guerrilla protest organization." The group, which has chapters in many states and counties, opposes all assaults on the Bill of Rights, but focuses on the right to keep and bear arms. Wherever anti-gunners are scheduled to speak, rally, march, issue a press release, or hold a news conference, the TRT aims to be there, adamant and highly visible.

Group members have worn yellow stars of David to show that gun owners in America are as demonized as Jews in Nazi Germany. They've digitally imposed the faces of gun banners onto photos of uniformed Nazi soldiers, accusing them of having a "Final Solution" for gun owners. They've disrupted anti-gunners picnics with bullhorns.

They aim, as Bob says, "to raise the price of tyranny" — to hold anti-freedom agents personally accountable. Politicians who've gotten used to perks and respect need to hear themselves publicly called thieves, liars, and fascists. "Fair-weather fighters" in the anti-gun movement need to know that it's not going to be so fun to turn up at that rally with the other soccer mommies. And it works.

If you want to do something highly visible to defend the Bill of Rights, and you'd enjoy a group that gets its enemies so upset that they either flee or stand around and make bloody idiots of themselves, consider the TRT.

The national Web site is www.trtnational.org/. Or type "Tyranny Response Team" into a good search engine.

A "No" uttered from deepest conviction is better and greater than a "Yes" merely uttered to please, or what is worse, to avoid trouble. — Mahatma Ghandi

23. Small steps

What if, when the bailiff called, "All rise!" you just didn't? What if, when addressing the judge, you carefully omitted the words, "Your Honor"?

Your *Honor*? Good grief! A judge is nothing but a combination of a lawyer and a politician. What on earth is likely to be honorable about that? If anybody's going to address anybody as "Your Honor" in this situation, the judge oughta address you that way. Even if you're a scum-sucking, embezzling, money-laundering, kitty-kicking tripper of little old ladies, you're probably more honorable than the black-robed government cultist sitting behind the bench!

The point of this little exercise, however (as writer Patty Neill pointed out), isn't to dis some specific judge. It's to help break any ancient conditioning that causes you to give automatic respect to authority. (And if we're honest with ourselves, most of us have such a lurking groveler in us, even if we like to believe otherwise.)

Don't refer to a politician as "The Honorable" even on the most formal of occasions. Call it by its first name if you happen to meet one socially. Give it neither attention nor glory. *Don't even give it the credence of criticizing it!* It's beneath your notice, a waste of your valuable time.

Obey a cop's orders if the situation calls for it, but when you meet a cop on the street or at your door, don't act as if it has some right to start ordering you around at will. Don't be nasty, but rid your demeanor of any groveling qualities or unearned respect.

Yes, there's the occasional judge who'll threaten you with contempt of court for not treating it like a lordling. There's also the more-than-occasional cop who *likes* people to tremble in its presence. But if you're simply polite, while refusing to grovel, most won't be corrupt enough to make an issue out of it. For practical information on how and when you can stand up for yourself, I highly recommend Boston T. Party's book, *You and the Police.*

Small steps. But if you regard yourself as anyone's equal, and behave as if you're anyone's equal, you've just taken an important step toward freeing your mind. You are becoming *more* than the equal of those who rely on uniforms and platforms for their superiority.

Extraordinary claims require extraordinary evidence. —Carl Sagan

24. Secrets of the conspiracy REVEALED!

oaiseroisyoernIpPDIU*(&@!!^!!@<g><g>@@)!)@*
&!!^!!@^(__kISSinger1-0q8q970qwerrrr087111BreszhinsK
Py8009723)&@!^   (!@!RELLEFEKCOR---------ohESO-
HT(&@!!(*!!@_!   nAStY!*(&!BANk-Sters@!JID-A7AP
807W   buTQRVA79   yLTSoMS8YOUR   9fEAr!!!-
&^(&@AER. :-) :-) :-) Why era uoy so deirrow tuoba tahw
they od, so ylsuoiretsym? Od nac *uoy* tahw no sucof!

Me... a skeptic? I trust you have proof...— Fidonet
tagli*ne*

25. The Chernalevsky Method

Here's a true story from my own experience. (Identifying details have been changed to protect the innocent, guilty, and just plain strange.)

There was once a prominent Connecticut psychoanalyst named Chernalevsky. He charged big bucks to rich suburbanites. They paid up and adored him. But Dr. Chernalevsky was rude enough to up and die one day, without notice. He keeled over and was gone.

Needless to say, some people with money and fragile psyches were devastated. One was so desperate to pour his heart out to the insightful Dr. Chernalevsky that... well, he just kept right on pouring his heart out to Dr. Chernalevsky. He continued holding regular — albeit figurative — sessions with the dead psychoanalyst, confessing away and listening for the doctor's replies.

Then the former patient, now well on the road to recovery, wrote a book entitled *The Chernalevsky Method*, recommending his dead-doctor technique to others, but giving credit where he believed it was due, to the shrink himself.

The doctor's daughter Maria sued the author. When she told me about this, I made sympathetic noises, then just had to ask, "Yeah, but does the method *work*?"

"Apparently it does," she confessed.

Draw your own conclusions.

> *We expect them to work toward the elimination of human rights, elimination of human rights in accordance with the pursuit of justice.* — Dan Quayle

26. Police-anoia: Or boy, these guys give us some great ideas!

The following memo, dated 9-18-97, appeared throughout Indiana State Police stations. It's real. Similar memos have circulated among officials in Washington state, California and elsewhere. These documents offer quite a revealing glimpse into how power lovers look upon people like thee and me.

I present Indiana's version here *in full*, with not one word deleted (with my commentary in italics), both as an example of the "hate literature" that passes for government documents these days and because, well, by golly, these nice cops explain in detail some real whiz-bang ideas for standing up to them! Here goes, with many thanks to the keep-'em-smiling officers of the Indiana State Police:

Threat Assessment of the Patriot Movement in Indiana
By Lt. Steven R. King of Indiana State Police

It's not THAT Stephen King, though this guy does write pretty scary copy.

Beginning with the bombing of the World Trade Center in New York City in February of 1993, the United States has come face-to-face with terrorism. What was once a foreign problem now is a matter to be dealt with by Americans on an almost daily basis.

Since 2001, this is true. But which is ultimately more dangerous? Terrorism, or a police state imposed in the name of fighting terrorism?

The growth of the right-wing Patriot Movement, in terms of its membership and activities, has been felt in Indiana as well as the rest of the nation.

Note the dazzling leap from the World Trade Center bombing to right-wing patriots. Um...uh...I don't recall them convicting any "right-wing" types for that one, do you?

The anti-government sentiment shared by the various components of the Patriot Movement (sovereign citizens, tax resisters, gun rights activists, citizens militias and common law courts) has become a growing concern of government officials and those in law enforcement. While present information does not lead law enforcement officials to believe that an offensive threat is being planned by members of the Patriot Movement in Indiana, this faction of society still poses a threat to the general public and government officials.

Let me get this straight. They're not threatening anybody, but you still feel threatened by them. Isn't there a word for that? Have you seen a shrink about this condition lately? Dr. Chernalevsky, maybe?

The Patriot Movement in Indiana consists (sic) of several pockets of activities spread throughout Indiana. There are approximately fifty counties that have some type of Patriot Movement activity. No part of the state is exempt from such right-wing groups.

Glad to hear it! Good for you Indianians.

The most prominent groups represent sovereign citizens, citizens militias and common law courts. Law enforcement officials can never discount that a violent event such as the bombing at Oklahoma City can never happen in Indiana.

Yep. And you can't discount that a meteor won't ever strike you on the head, either. But whatever happened to looking for evidence of a problem before you panic about it?

But the most likely event to occur in Indiana involving the Patriot Movement will more than likely be in the form of a confrontation or stand-off. This could occur as the result of a traffic stop, during the service of official legal documents or as the result of attempting to take a person into custody. There are several visible trends that point to this type of event.

My goodness, Lt. King just said something accurate for a change! These are the exact circumstances under which confrontations are likely to occur. However, he never seems to consider that people wouldn't be so up in arms if they knew the cops were never going to search them illegally, hassle them because of their views, arrest them for victimless crimes, subject them to civil forfeiture, entrap them into committing statutory crimes, then railroad them through a corrupt court system. Hey, Mr. King, were "confrontations" or "standoffs" common in the days when people understood what the law was and believed they could get justice in the courts?

One growing trend among members of the Patriot Movement is to not carry a drivers license or have legal vehicle registration plates. Instead, these individuals will carry home made permits that grant them the authority to "travel the common ways as a private Christian."

Well, I'm not sure what a "private Christian" might be, or why a private agnostic or a private pagan doesn't qualify for a permit. But nevertheless, good for them for questioning authority.

It is highly likely that such individuals will present a "Public Servants Questionnaire" to the police officer when initially stopped for a traffic violation. The violator will refuse to answer questions related to the traffic stop until the officer responds to a series of twenty-two questions related to information files that may be maintained on the subject. This is done under a loose interpretation of the Privacy Act of 1974. The Privacy Act of 1974, and subsequent amendments, is to prevent government agencies from maintaining secret files on citizens. This presents an interesting situation where someone with an anti-government stand is attempting to use laws enacted by the Federal government to protect their rights.

Now, this is where it starts to get really interesting. Can anyone tell me why state cops should feel threatened by people using laws to protect their rights?????

There are many documented cases in Indiana where traffic violators have presented such home made permits to officers. There is also a growing trend in Indiana where officers, especially along interstate routes, are seeing truck drivers based in Western states carrying such permits instead of a drivers license.

Interesting. Thanks for the tip.

Another trend involving traffic stops has the violator holding their drivers license and registration, if they actually have them, up at the window for the officer to see but not take. This stems from an interpretation of the law requiring individuals to "identify" themselves. Some courts in Indiana have ruled that the act of holding the drivers license and vehicle registration at the window for the officer to view meets the intent of that law. Therefore, according to the courts, the officer has no need to take the license and registration back to their vehicle for the purpose of writing a traffic citation.

Whoops, there my feeble little brain goes again, having trouble understanding the problem. Lessee...Your very own courts say they can hold up their ID in this way. But when they do, it becomes part of this big "threat" you're worried about. Obeying the law. It threatens you. I'm sorry, readers. I'm sure a lawyer could explain why the cops are so scared of people obeying the law, but I can't.

There is one final thought concerning traffic stops. The Indiana State Police has had several instances where Patriot Movement members stopped for a traffic violation have contacted other Patriot Movement members by radio and had them come to the scene of the traffic stop. While not exiting their vehicle to approach the officer, their presence is very obvious. This presents two concerns for the officer. The first is that all Patriot Movement members will most likely be armed, and there is more than likely a video camera recording the event. The best the members of the Patriot Movement can hope for is the officer to violate their constitutional rights and then have grounds for a civil suit against the officer and the agency. If successful, that type of news would spread around the nation like wild fire.

Okay, I'll try again. Citizens peacefully observing police activity is a problem. *The mere presence of both guns and* video cameras *(!) is a problem. Well, have I got a solution for you, boys! Just don't violate anybody's rights and you won't have a thing to worry about!*

Another situation that could result in a stand-off may result from the attempted service of legal documents. Since those in the Patriot Movement do not recognize the legal authority of the Federal and State government, they will resist any attempt at enforcement of legal documents from such courts. Such resistance can occur no matter whether the documents are part of a criminal or civil proceeding. A stand-off in Jefferson County in 1995, [which] involved Patriot member Mark Adams, stemmed from a custody battle and the fact that Adams did not recognize the authority of the local court or the county sheriff. The stand-off between Adams, supported by militia members, and local and state law enforcement officers lasted for several hours before being brought to a peaceful resolution.

Though I'm not among those who get into the legal arcana of jurisdictions and standing, I wonder if these State Police can show a constitutional justification for every act they commit. And if they can't...then who's got the bigger problem?

Another trend that is sure to increase involves the use of "paper terrorism" or "nuisance terrorism."

This is just an all-time fave. Issuing paper documents or asking too many questions being equated with blowing babies up with bombs! Of course, since the police and their government cronies are often the "victims," they like to exaggerate their plight.

This brand of terrorism is often conducted by the common law courts and sovereign citizen factions of the Patriot Movement. This includes the filing of bogus liens against property of public officials, to include police officers.

If putting a false lien on someone's property is such a bad thing — which it definitely is — how come the prisons aren't filled with IRS agents, sheriffs and bankers? How come its only a problem when "civilians" do it?

While not having a financial claim against the property holder, the intent of the lien filing is more directed at the inconvenience caused when the property holder attempts to sell the property only to find a claim against the property. Since a clear title of property is required in order to complete a sale of property, it is the responsibility of the property holder to prove that there is no basis for the lien. That means court and legal fees being incurred by the property holder to prove the lien is frivolous. The attempted filing of such liens has been attempted on several occasions by Patriot groups through the Secretary of State's office. This is a tactic that will very likely increase over the next several months.

Outside of Indiana, a Patriot group filed a W-2 form with the Internal Revenue Service on a police officer that the group felt was harassing them. The tax filing was for alleged consulting work done by the officer for the Patriot group with a $10,000 fee paid to the officer. When the officer did not claim that income on his tax return, nor pay the tax, the IRS investigated the matter. It was the responsibility of the officer to clear his name and prove that he had in fact never performed the consulting work nor received the income claimed by the Patriot group.

Snort. Chuckle. A clever friend points out that someone could compound this trick by submitting a W-2, or a 1099 Form (compensation to independent contractors) not in the name of his own group, but in the name, and under the taxpayer ID number, of a company or individual engaged in offensive activities. Might get them in trouble, too.

One tactic that officers should be aware of involves attempts by Patriot groups to discredit the officer's credit rating. A number of tactics can be employed that will result in a bad credit rating for the officer.

Remember the days when good, law-abiding people regarded police officers as their friends? *Notice how these policifers are entirely neglecting to ask* why *people calling themselves patriots would feel driven to such dirty tactics?*

Some Patriot Movement groups are becoming more involved in government at the local level. Two county commissioners won election in a central Indiana county last November with a great amount of support from the local citizens militia.

Ohmigod! You mean these dangerous lunatics are even voting??? *Hang 'em! Fry 'em! This has to be stopped before it goes any further!!!*

Since there are only three county commissioners, the citizens militia feels that they own the two commissioners they supported.

Would the police say something like this if a police organization had worked to elect two officials?

Actions by the commissioners have resulted in the abolishment of all county zoning ordinances and taking a stand against recycling.

Excuse me. I think I'm going to faint. I simply can't bear any more of these shocks. What depravity these Patriots practice! Taking a stand against...recycling! Opposing...zoning! Those commie pinko weirdo fascist lunatic anarchist ravening savage hordes! Stomp 'em all. Annihilate 'em! Save our daughters from a fate worse than death at the hands of such monsters!

Twice a resolution has been presented at a commissioners meeting that would mandate all property owners in the county to own a firearm for protection.

Presented. While as a libertarian I can't advocate the "mandating" of ownership of anything, I rather like the spirit. But, um, if those vile Patriots "own" two out of three of the commissioners...how come that sucker didn't pass?

A new citizens militia has recently started in west Central Indiana with a reserve city police officer serving as the leader.

Smile.

On the bright side to the Patriot Movement, recently some high profile leaders in Indiana have either left the state or are serving jail time. Indianapolis attorney and self-proclaimed "Adjutant General of the Militia" Linda Thompson has moved to Alabama. Tax resister Joe Holland from Warrick County is serving time in connection to convictions in Federal court on various fraud related charges. The leader of the Freeman group in Kosciusko County is serving time for non-payment of court ordered child support that he attempted to make restitution for with a bad check. This has left a void to some degree in the leadership of the Patriot Movement in Indiana.

While the likelihood of a violent act in Indiana related to the Patriot Movement seems remote, law enforcement must not let its guard down against such groups. We must be constantly vigilant to the "nuisance tactics" attempted by such anti-government groups.

While we let murderers, rapists, tax collectors and bureaucrats run loose.

A twenty-one year veteran of the Indiana State Police, Lt. Steven R. King is commander of the Field Operations Section in the Enforcement Division at General Headquarters in Indianapolis. In that capacity, Lt. King serves as the agency's liaison to the State Emergency Management Agency and is actively involved in response planning related to a potential terrorist attack. Lt. King is a member of the Indiana Terrorist Task Force, serving as co-chair of the Training committee. A certified instructor by the I.L.E.T.B., Lt. King has presented many training programs related to terrorism for the State Police, FBI, US Justice Department, local government and local law enforcement officers. Topics for such training have included planning a response to a terrorist's incident, the ideology and philosophy of right-wing groups, the militia movement and the use of potential weapons of mass destruction.

In other words, with all these terrorism tasks on his plate, he has to come up with something to justify his existence and his budgets. Pretty thin stuff, Mr. King. Pretty thin. Nevertheless, thanks for the ideas.

There is not a single large institution...in the world today that is satisfactorily performing all of the functions people have assigned to it. They are creaking, cracking, and even crashing under their own weight... Yet people themselves persist, contrive to survive, even make things better; and more and more they do all of those things with less and less direct reference to the major institutions. People seem to be going one way, institutions another. — Karl Hess, Community Technology

27. Everything you need

Would you like to save money, pay less to the government, and quit supporting a corporate culture that regards you as nothing but a mindless "consumer"? Then just remember that, sooner or later, everything you ever need will show up at a:

- Garage sale
- Second-hand store
- Grocery store dumpster
- Farmer's market
- Flea market
- Charity store
- Food co-op
- Barter meet

- Friend's house
- Used car lot
- Illegal country dumpsite
- Vacant lot or vacant house
- Antique store
- Farm
- Landfill
- Gun show
- Craft show

A tedious way to acquire the things you want? I thought so at first. That is, until I caught the thrill of the honey-for-books swap, the found-in-the-woods oak bed, and the $7.50 reloading press. Every time I'm tempted to go the instant gratification route again, I ask myself, "Cui bono?" I tell you, it ain't you and me who benefits from those trips to Nordstrom's and the Chevy dealer. Not in the long run.

Oh yeah, business is good for America. But despite all that stuff we learned in school about economies of scale and the modern miracle of the assembly line, big, corporate business isn't good for anything but itself and its circle-jerk buddies in Washington, D.C. If good business is like a hard-working, loving dog, corporate business is like Godzilla.

There is something to be said for business by and for human beings. Something about the way it promotes freedom. Read Karl Hess' *Community Technology* (first published in 1979, and recently re-issued by Loompanics Unlimited, with an introduction by Carol Moore) for deeper thoughts on that. The book is probably too starry-eyed and idealistic, but it sure gives a different perspective on business and its role in our lives than the one we learned in government schools.

If one sets aside time for a business appointment or shopping expedition, that time is inviolable. But if one says, "I cannot come because that is my hour to be alone," one is considered rude, egotistical or strange.

What a commentary on our civilization. — Anne Morrow Lindbergh

28. The joys of being independently poor

When you *don't want to be poor*, poverty sucks. But when you embrace poverty with the fervor of a nun, it can be a blessing, a challenge, a creative state and the best thing that ever happened to you.

Sometime when I was in my 20s I noticed that, during times when I had a bit of money, money became very important to me. I'd spend it all. I'd think about how to spend it. I'd spend time budgeting and counting and anticipating it. Worst of all I'd suddenly notice that my couch or my car or my closet was desperately lacking and in need of *instant* attention. Then I'd go out and buy what I wanted — and buy even more, on credit! On the other hand, during times when the money didn't flow, I discovered I didn't need, or even want, much beyond necessities. It wasn't that I was "doing without." It was just that I was living without money as my focus. It didn't take me long to notice which was the happier state.

I also know the other kind of poverty. I know what it's like to have to choose between paying the bills and buying groceries. Not pleasant — and less so when others rely on you. But frankly, I'd rather be in that state than in the state of having too much. It may not be fun, but boy, it keeps you in touch with what's important in life — something people quickly lose when they think "important" means having the latest-model Mercedes!

For many of us "shruggers" (Item 40), it has become philosophically important to remain poor. For tax resisters, it's a helpful way of becoming an unattractive target. For many others, today and in the near future, refusal to accept Universal Citizen Numbering or to be databased to death will virtually assure us lives of poverty (or at least, of great financial risk) outside the system. Insecure as this can be (What do I do if my car breaks down? What if I get sick? How do I send my kids to college?), we can find ways to enjoy it and benefit from chosen or enforced poverty. Try to find creativity in doing without. Work for freedom instead of dollars.

> *It is not enough for law to be meticulous, it must also be just. It is not enough for law to be meticulous and just, it must be understanding. It is not enough for law to be meticulous, just and understanding, it must also be compassionate. It is not enough for law to be meticulous, just, understanding and compassionate, it must be rooted in absolute truth. If man is to rise above mere beasthood then he must obey just law, formulated by just men. I repeat, just law, formulated by just men, and not random and expedient law which is the servant of tyrants.* — Marcus Tullius Cicero

29. Your banker is NOT your friend

Now, here's a cute one. Did you know that your banker is actually eligible for a cut of the goods if he, she or it reports you to the feds for making "suspicious" transactions and the feds seize your assets as a result? I noted in the original *101 Things* that your banker could be fined for failing to guess if you were making "suspicious" transactions.[10] Bankers must

---

[10] According to *John Pugley's Journal*, December 1996, "The derelict bank employee can be criminally prosecuted and faces $250,000 in fines and 5 years in jail. If the Feds decide a banker has engaged in 'willful blindness' towards what

fill out Suspicious Activity Reports if they guess you're up to something. But I didn't know the half of it then. That friendly little teller smiling across the counter is just *hoping* you'll do something "suspicious" so she can earn a cut of the loot — up to 25 percent of any fine or forfeiture levied against you!

Remember, too, "suspicious" can include any cash transaction(s) with a cumulative value of at least $5,000. "Suspicious" is almost entirely in the eye of the beholder. But at www.occ.treas.gov/launder/orige.htm, the Treasury Department's own site, you'll find several lists of the things bankers are trained to be on the lookout for — things like "depositing musty or extremely dirty bills," "exchanging small bills for large bills or vice versa," "sudden changes in banking patterns," "nervous" customers, and customers who "refuse to provide any other information the bank requires to open an account." If you have any cash at all, that smiling little teller has every incentive to manufacture "suspicions" against you. And with new "customer profiling" methods, the teller won't even have to bother. The bank's computers will recognize "suspicious" patterns or transactions and report you to the feds automatically!

But don't be nervous about that, dear little bank customers. Remember, only "suspicious" people are nervous. Smile real nice at that little teller now, and look as much like Ward or June Cleaver as you can — then get your money the hell out of federal banks and into some other place and form.

But don't take it anywhere in cash. Having cash, as we know, is prima facie evidence of drug dealing.

---

the Feds think should be suspect customer conduct, the banker faces special punishment of $500,000 in fines and 10 years in prison."

Ain't it funny how the bankers make out... the feds make out...the state agencies that mimic the feds make out. The courts make out, the prisons make out, the lawyers make out? And the alleged drug dealers and terrorists— against whom all this is supposedly directed — just go right along with business as usual. Everybody makes out it seems but you, me and the Lady in the Harbor.

> *Authorities are now saying that the war on drugs will be bigger than World War II... oh, great,* more *Time-Life books.* — Jay Leno

30. Hey, they'll do it to you...

In its June 22, 1998 issue, *Time* magazine printed a blurb — in its frothy little "People" section, of all places, headed "Patty's Paranoia Pays Off."

Piecing together the *Time* story and a more complete one that appeared June 9, 1998 in the New York *Post*, we come up with this: In February 1998, the famous heiress, Patty Hearst Shaw, received a mysterious package at her home in Connecticut. The package bore a San Diego postmark and two phone numbers. Something about it bothered her, so she left it on the porch while she went inside to call the numbers. Both numbers turned out to be pay phones. That confirmed her suspicions, and she immediately called police.

Within minutes, federal DEA agents showed up. No, they weren't responding to her police call. (Though they were certainly alerted by her two calls to what must have been signal numbers.) They were there to arrest her for receiving the package, which they said contained many thousands of dollars worth of an unspecified illegal drug. But since Hearst had already phoned the police, the DEA couldn't arrest her for receiving drugs, as they had planned to do. Had Hearst delayed her phone call to the police by just half an hour, she'd have gone to jail on federal drug charges. Now, you tell me the DEA didn't set that up.

Hearst believes the DEA or the federal Justice Department *did* set it up in response to her application for a presidential pardon — which had come up for DOJ review just two weeks earlier. (Hearst, if you remember, was kidnapped by the Symbionese Liberation Army back in the seventies, and later convicted of crimes she committed in company with her kidnappers. She claims her participation in crimes was coerced.) Hearst's lawyer, George Martinez, was quoted in the *Post* as saying the DEA was conducting a "campaign of harassment" against his client. He has asked Janet Reno to investigate. (Yeah, Janet Reno's a real champ about investigating government corruption, isn't she?)

The *Post* also quotes Hearst as saying, "I can't think of a more horrible, more insidious way to ruin someone's reputation. I don't know who sent it, [but] it had to be someone with access to large amounts of narcotics who doesn't have to pay for them....I was left with the notion never to let federal agents back into my house again... It's like a friend said, it's like being caught in an episode of *The X-Files*."

As the *Post* so eloquently stated, "The DEA did not return a call for comment."

Now, imagine: If the DEA has enough brass to try to frame a wealthy celebrity who can afford the best lawyers on the planet, and the media considers it nothing more than an amusing "people" blurb, how many thousands of poor schmucks are in prison right now on exactly the same kind of frame-ups?

Two lessons: Watch your butt if you've ever done anything to make "law enforcement" mad at you; and remember that when you're dealing with government enforcers you're dealing with people utterly without ethics or human decency. It'll be no surprise when some freedom lovers give them a taste of their own medicine.

Chapter Two

In this chapter we move on to more action-oriented items. Some are symbolic, some practical. Some safe, some not-so-safe. Something for every freedom fan, I hope.

31. 419

In August 1998, I was a guest on the radio show, "Tim Kern: Talking Sense," on the American Freedom Network. Tim was a delightful host, and I was having a great time, but I was puzzled by all the callers who began and ended their messages, "Four-nineteen, Tim!"

It was a great, jaunty salute. I recognized it as the famous date on which so many events significant in the history of freedom and tyranny have occurred. But I didn't know why they were using it as a greeting. Later, I asked Tim, and he told me this:

> Actually, I got the idea from Che Guevara's "26 Julio" movement; but his date had far less significance and coincidence of events.
>
> I, and a few other talk show hosts who have joined me, use it like "Aloha," either as "hello" or "good-bye." I intended for it to be a Patriot greeting, sort of like a fraternity handshake. Here's an article I wrote about it... Adapted from "The Americans' Fight to Survive," by Gunnery Sergeant

---

Red Smith with Tim Kern (Available from the American Freedom Network, 1-800-205-6245):

419

Pronounced "four-nineteen," this greeting and symbol is the mark of the American freedom movement. It commemorates a date which is etched into the memories of Americans: the date (1993) of the final assault on Waco, Texas. Other important events associated with April 19 and tyranny include the shot heard 'round the world at Concord Bridge (1775), President Lincoln's naval blockade of the United States' southern ports (1861), the final assault on the Jewish Warsaw ghetto (1943), the coup d'etat in Laos (1964), and the terrible Oklahoma City bombing (1995).

When Americans get together, "419" can substitute for any standard greeting, thus identifying Americans concerned with the restoration of the Constitution, Americans who will, if need be, resist tyranny, through their cooperation and support of one another. As a number on a cap, as a cryptic bumper sticker, or as white numbers on a flag-blue armband, it identifies one who will, if necessary, commit his whole being to the protection and defense of the Constitution from all its enemies, foreign and domestic. ...In short, it represents hope, faith, and a total commitment to the principles which guarantee the brightest future for all who subscribe to it: the Constitution of the United States of America. 419, Americans!

There are four types of homicide: felonious, excusable, justifiable, and praiseworthy. — Ambrose Bierce

32. Bill of Rights Enforcement

From time to time, somebody comes up with *the* magic bullet — the one, single, pure, pluperfect action they believe will sweep away tyranny and restore liberty to the land. If only everyone would get behind it. If only Congress would implement it.

They may propose wiping out all but the first 13 amendments to the Constitution — or passing one comprehensive new one. Returning to the ancient tariff system. Mounting a nationwide, grassroots effort to restore the citizen legislature. Abolishing private funding of political campaigns. Holding a new continental congress. Whatever. It would free the nation, they assure us. Entirely free it. In one single, dramatic, nonviolent action. If only...if only...

One of the most painful parts of the stand for freedom is watching these hopeful souls make hopeful presentations of their hopeless causes — while tyranny continues to march. If only ...if only. But it's never to be. Most of the ideas actually wouldn't accomplish what their supporters hope. But they'll never get the chance to find out because the hopefully hopeless ideas will go absolutely nowhere.

I've heard of only one such magic bullet that actually could strike the tyrant to the heart if it were carried out. While it's *probably* just as doomed as all the others, it has two advantages:

- It really *would* assure freedom, if it were implemented. It wouldn't merely create a different kind of administrative, centralized nightmare, as some other "solutions" would;

- And, in part, at least, we can implement it ourselves, without waiting eternally for Congress to get a freedom clue.

The idea, brilliant in its simplicity, is Bill of Rights Enforcement. Writer L. Neil Smith came up with it and he and friends have built a World Wide Web campaign around it. Just enforce the entire Bill of Rights — straight down the line, from Article I to Article X, without quibble. No need for huge, expensive, nationwide efforts to create something new. Just enforce the old.

Liberals, learn to live with the Second Amendment if you want others to defend your precious First. Flag lovers, realize free people are able to burn flags, however repugnant it may be to you. Defend their First Amendment, and they'll defend your Second. Scrupulously fair criminal trials? Yep, even when the guy on trial is a thoroughgoing bastard. Right to privacy? Right to blitz your brain with dope without interference from a federal agency? Yep, it's clearly covered in Article IX. Hey, we won't let the feds seize your nature preserve if you won't let them seize our cash (Article IV). Tell the feds to stay out of our states! (Article X) Jury trial for *all* criminal cases, even petty ones? You bet! (Article VI) Article X alone wipes away nearly everything that the federal government has imposed in the last 40 years. And Article IX takes care of most of the rest. And yeah, if anybody tries to quarter soldiers on you in time of peace, the only so-far unviolated amendment, you have a right to slam the door in their faces (Article III).

Though I really don't think Bill of Rights Enforcement will ever be implemented across the land — both because "the government" will never enforce laws that deprive it of power, and because most individuals will remain more than willing to take others' rights, while still demanding their own — there's still some hope in that we, freedom-loving individuals, can take *some* steps to enforce the Bill of Rights in our own lives. Maybe, often, we have to do it covertly or at risk to ourselves. Maybe sometimes we'll have to face public condemnation in doing it. Our efforts will never be sufficient to free the nation. But we can begin without waiting for others to join us, or for anyone to contribute money, build an organization or pass a law.

One thing we can absolutely do is to educate ourselves and others about what the Bill contains, what it really means, and why each and every human being — even the ones we don't like — deserves the Bill's protection. Jews for the Preservation of Firearms Ownership is one organization promoting comprehensive Bill of Rights consciousness. Please note that JPFO's effort is *not* associated with Neil Smith's — though they are complementary. Part of what JPFO is dedicated to — getting governments to pass Bill of Rights Day declarations — is also too symbolic for words. (Well, actually, it's so symbolic it's *just* words. Of *course* governments are in favor of the Bill of Rights — just like they're in favor of freedom, fidelity, family, religion and truth — in theory.)

Nevertheless, between what Neil and his friends are up to and what Aaron Zelman and JPFO are doing, here's a beginning, for those who still have hope:

Jews for the Preservation of Firearms Ownership
P.O. Box 270143
Hartford, WI 53207
voice: (262) 673-9745
fax: (262) 673-9746
e-mail: webmaster@jpfo.org
www.jpfo.org

Inquire about their excellent Gran'pa Jack cartoon pamphlets. These contain lucid and principled Bill of Rights education for school children. Some focus on firearms, but at least one covers the entire Bill of Rights and does it brilliantly.

Neil Smith's Bill of Rights Enforcement campaign on the Internet, including background information and graphics for Web masters is found at:

www.lneilsmith.com/bor_enforcement.html

It's like an Alcatraz around my neck. — A former mayor of Boston

33. On shunning

Shunning is the ancient art of shutting individuals out of a group, thoroughly, publicly and without mercy. It has historically been a potent weapon to intimidate agents of an oppressor or pressure collaborators into changing their ways.

American colonials called it "discountenancing" when they refused to trade with, socialize or even speak with advocates of the Stamp Act, the Townshend Acts and other British outrages.

During a 19th century rent strike, the British government stationed policemen in the town of Kilmallock, Ireland. Britain, however, neglected to provide these agents with transportation. Innkeepers refused them horses and carriages. Shopkeepers refused to sell them food, rendering them helpless and vulnerable. Again, in the turmoil between the Easter Uprising of 1916 and the victory of the Irish Republic, people all across Ireland boycotted the enemy Royal Irish Constabulary. "A policy of ostracism, including the refusal to sell food to the members, demoralized the force more than a few murders or the threat of more; the men were mostly Irish and resigned in large numbers, and no new recruits came forward."[1] During World War II, the Polish resistance sentenced to "infamy" anyone who collaborated with the Nazis.

---

[1] Charles L. Mowat, *Britain Between the Wars: 1918 to 1940*, as quoted in *The Politics of Nonviolent Action, Part Two, The Methods of Nonviolent Action*, by Gene Sharp, Extending Horizons Books, Boston, 1973.

No one would patronize their businesses; their names were published and circulated, and after the war, some of them were tried as criminals. Even today, groups such as the Amish use shunning as a powerful weapon to bring dissenters into line or drive them out of the community.

As we seek effective means to thwart tyrants — means somewhere between the useless ballot box and the inflammatory cartridge box — is shunning a technique we should explore to help break the agents of tyranny?

Shunning is more difficult today than it was in the past:

- It's more effective in small communities than in vast societies;
- Mobility also makes it difficult, particularly if the target is a federal employee who can simply be rotated out of an assignment if things get too intense;
- There are a hodgepodge of laws that make it illegal to refuse to serve or associate with protected classes of people;

That said, however, shunning still has a certain power. It strikes at the very heart of human nature — the desire to belong. It evokes one of the most primitive of fears — that of being turned upon by other members of the flock.

Shunning is nonviolent. But in some ways it's more cruel than taking a shotgun to your enemy. A shotgun is quick. But when the bad cop, the federal bureaucrat, the DEA agent, the boyfriend of the local commissar can't even show its face in public without seeing other faces turned away in contempt, its whole life becomes a misery.

Shunning may even take more ruthlessness on your part than it would take to apply a shotgun to an oppressor's anatomy. In part that's because shunning logically extends to the families, friends and associates of the guilty individuals, as well. If you're going to do it properly, shunning means that your six-year-old won't play with your target's kids. It means *you* won't be nice to those innocent little kids. You'll chase them off your property, snarl if they come selling cookies, walk out when they turn up at a recital or school play, and do everything you can to make *them* as miserable as their guilty parent.

Go out of your way to make little kids miserable, just because mommy or daddy is a tax collector? Rotten, right? But necessary if you are to make shunning work. Miserable, confused children and spouses apply pressure to the target even where you can't — in the home. Making them miserable completes the task of making the target's life untenable.

For shunning to be effective:

- It must be all-pervasive; a majority, or at least an impressive minority, of the community (neighborhood, company, church, whatever) must turn on the villain.

- No shunner should *ever* give the target — or his family — a break. Nobody must ever let the pressure off and invite the guy for a beer or invite the woman to a movie. The effort must be total and unyielding.

- Even if storekeepers, restaurant owners and other business people feel they must serve the target to avoid being shut down or sued, they should do it as coldly, inefficiently, and with as many unpleasantries as they can dream up. (Spill the soup in the IRS agent's lap; "lose" the legislator's order.) Make it very clear the target isn't welcome anywhere.

- Shunning must be unyielding. It doesn't stop until the target goes away, quits the offensive job, changes attitude or otherwise stops doing the objectionable thing.

There is *no* way out except for the shunned agent of the oppressor to stop committing oppression.

While in some senses it *is* more difficult to shun in this mass, mobile society, communications have also made it easier in other senses — just different. For instance, when a cop's corruption or brutality is revealed on the Internet or in the print Samizdat, the word quickly goes nationwide. While it isn't possible for an old lady in Seattle to refuse to serve cookies to a state cop in Illinois, she can certainly make him feel vulnerable in other ways, such as discreetly publicizing information about him.

Shunning is *not* physically attacking. It is *not* killing the target's cat. (Shame on anyone who even thinks of such things!) It is *not* breaking her windows or putting a rattlesnake in his mailbox. Shunning is strictly a social punishment. It is always and entirely nonviolent. Shunning is the eye turned away in contempt, the unaccountable bad service in every store, the refusal to sit in the same pew in church...these are the techniques of shunning. Nonviolent, but unrelenting.

Who can be shunned?

- Every IRS employee on the planet;
- Every BATF agent or employee;
- Members of other unconstitutional and/or abusive federal police agencies: DEA, FBI, INS, etc.;
- Other bureaucrats employed by freedom-destroying state or federal agencies;
- Local officials who cooperate with abusive federal agencies;
- State legislators who bend over and pass the enabling legislation for federal Big Brother laws;

- Workers who carry out anti-freedom instructions (e.g. equipment operators who close roads on "public" land);

- Even low-level bureaucrats who enforce injustice. (Anyone who claims, or is in a position to claim, "I was only following orders.");

- If it comes to this — members of military or other "emergency" occupying forces who are acting illegally.

Resistance is futile! You must obey!

34. Staging a comply-in

Before I quit borrowing from Gene Sharp, let me mention one more tactic from his fine book, *The Methods of Nonviolent Action.* This one's called "a comply-in." To perform it, you and your allies merely conform with every miniscule requirement of an objectionable law. Sharp gives the example of draft protestors circa 1970.

The Selective Service Law required draft registrants to notify their draft boards within ten days of any change of address "or status." A little-known aspect of the law also extended this requirement to men clear up in middle-age, not just draft-eligible young men. So protesters began to flood draft boards with written notifications of their changes in status, notifications such as: "This is to inform you that I've converted to Catholicism." "I'm hereby notifying you that I've moved my belongings from the back bedroom of my house to the front bedroom." "Please note that I've just broken up with my girlfriend." "My son has been promoted from lead technician to manager at Zowology Corporation." As you can see by that last item, the protesters also encouraged wives, girlfriends and daughters to notify draft boards of changes of status of the men in their lives. Some draft boards were soon buried — not only in this incoming dross, but in the acknowledgments they were required by law to mail back.

So, is there some obnoxious zoning law or planning board edict that technically requires you to submit an application each time you plant a daisy? Then by all means, submit! Do any tax laws, business licensing regulations, board certification procedures, vehicle registration laws or other intrusions on your freedom "require" you to flood bureaucrats with paperwork? Then, of course you should do your civic duty! Flood away!

Just one caution. This sort of thing is now lumped in the category of "paper terrorism." (As if your compliance with the law could be as threatening as a government-constructed bomb!) It may make you unpopular, get you put on lists and, above all, make you a target of investigation or retaliation by pissed off people with powerful pals. It's best done, and most safely done, when large numbers join you.

If problems ensue, you'll at least have the greatest defense of all. Wide-eyed and innocent, you can truly proclaim, "I was only obeying the law!"

CIVIL RIGHTS ACT
42 USC Chapter 21, Subchapter I, Section 1983

Civil action for deprivation of rights — Every person who, under color of any statute, ordinance, regulation, custom, or usage, of any State or Territory or the District of Columbia, subjects, or causes to be subjected, any citizen of the United States or other person within the jurisdiction thereof to the deprivation of any rights,

---

*privileges, or immunities secured by the Constitution
and laws, shall be liable to the party injured in an action at law, suit in equity, or other proper proceeding
for redress. (R.S. Sec. 1979, Public Law 96-170, Sec.
1, December 29, 1979, 93 State. 1284)*

35. Carl Drega: sad sign of the future

On August 19, 1997, a 67-year-old New Hampshire car-
penter, Carl Drega, was pulled over by police, apparently for
the crime of having rust holes in his pickup truck. For decades, Drega had been at odds with local officials. They had
accused him of zoning violations for his failure to finish a
building on time. They had dragged him into court for restor-
ing 80 feet of shoreline on his property after a storm had
washed it away. For all those decades, Drega had tried to
work within the system, getting permits, arguing in court,
pleading his case before boards of officials. And always losing. That August day, Drega had had enough. He would play
the system game no more. He blew away the two policemen
who had stopped him. Then he sought out his long-time chief
opponent, former town selectman, now judge, Vickie Bun-
nell, and shot her in the back as she fled. When the local
newspaper editor tried to stop him by wrapping his arms
around Drega's legs, Drega first warned him to, "Mind your
own fucking business." Then, when the editor continued to
hang on, Drega shot and killed him, too. Drega himself was
later killed by police. The story of these shootings, their pre-
liminaries and their aftermath has been eloquently told by
Vin Suprynowicz.

No doubt Carl Drega was an obsessive, difficult man in the
first place. As Vin points out, and I know from my own experience, every newspaper and every crusading writer hears

from them all the time. They plead for justice, not knowing how the real world works. They misinterpret legal rulings and misread paperwork. They brood over small slights and are driven mad over larger ones. I doubt Drega was a pleasant man to know, or a particularly rational one, even before his blow against his enemies. But had they simply left him alone, he'd have left them alone. Unfortunately, leaving people alone is a foreign concept to governments, these days.

How many more Dregas?

Since then, there have been more Carl Dregas. In 2000, California meat packer Stuart Anderson shot three government plant inspectors to death. They had closed his plant for health violations, even though his family-owned company had been in business 89 years without a single customer health problem. In Texas, rancher Melvin Edison Hale killed a state trooper who'd pulled him over for a seat-belt violation. In Texas, troopers can throw you in jail for not wearing a seat belt, and this was Hale's second "offense." In Bunker, Missouri, Gary Watson killed two men and wounded two others. They were city workers, on his property against his express will.

If we aren't able to take positive steps toward freedom — and soon — we're going to see a lot more of these people. The frustration is reaching the cracking point. We work and work and work for freedom. And not only do we not move forward, we are pushed eternally and brutally backward — gun registration, federal agents committing blatant murder and walking away with medals in their pockets, one new federal database after another, more regulations, more laws, more ordinary activities turned into crimes, more doors kicked in in the middle of the night, more random roadblocks, more property seized.

When we protest it all, we're simply dismissed as "haters," "gun-nuts," and "extremists." No one in the mainstream media or government listens to what we're saying long enough to recognize that we have a point. So the frustration increases.

We must either 1) see some major victories for the cause of freedom and major signals of the decline of government or 2) come up with things to do that give us the well-founded belief that we are assuring our own individual freedom in an unfree world. And we must do one or both of these things very, very soon. Or we'll not only see more Carl Dregas, but may see much worse, as desperate people explode in frustration.

The tyrants never understand, though. They never hear the message, even though it's clear and simple: Get out of our way. So *we* must understand. We must understand that they're never going to listen, so it's up to us to make our own freedom, where we can — outside their system. We must make the plans for it. We must pursue those plans, ourselves. And, if we possibly can, we need to channel some of our potential Dregas into some productive underground, extra-system activity so that their frustration won't have the chance to explode all over the freedom movement, doing more harm to us than to the tyrants.

These are the times that try men's souls. The summer soldier and the sunshine patriot will, in the crisis, shrink from the service of their country; but he that stands now, deserves the love and thanks of man and woman. Tyranny, like hell, is not easily conquered; yet we have this consolation with us, that the harder the conflict, the more glorious the triumph. What we ob-

tain too cheap, we esteem too lightly; 'tis dearness only that gives everything its value. Heaven knows how to put a proper price on its goods; and it would be strange indeed, if so celestial an article as freedom should not be highly rated. — Thomas Paine

36. Handling the rage

All we want is freedom and justice for every individual. Simple things to ask, you'd think, but impossible ones in this world where raw power is king, emperor and pope. And so the rage builds.

Of course the rage will explode somewhere. In the Drega-people, it already is exploding. But those of us who are goal-oriented, or patient, or just plain incurably *sensible* aren't going to let ourselves go take pot-shots at judges and IRS agents (however much they may merit it). We aren't going to immolate ourselves in the public plaza at high noon like a Buddhist monk, or open fire like a loony in a tower. We aren't going to go bonkers with frustration because going bonkers isn't a useful thing to do.

But what the hell are we going to do until it is time to let that righteous rage loose? Try this. Each time you encounter some outrage you can't do anything effective about, immediately do something truly effective *elsewhere*. For instance, when you learn about some poor grandmother 1,000 miles away having her house taken by cops because a grandson sold stolen radios from his bedroom, you can't fix that. But you can channel the rage into a variety of productive activities.

In Item 16, we looked at some very personal ways to help you handle frustration. This time, let's look at some specific (and as the bureaucrats love to say, "proactive") ways to di-

---

rectly help injured individuals or help the larger cause of freedom. Some of the following are perfectly legal. Some are legal, but risky. And some would be highly frowned upon by those who believe all law is good law. So again, measure your conscience, and consider anything you're uncomfortable with to be a far-out fantasy. You could:

- Start making a list of local officers and officials who carry out or profit from civil asset seizures. Gather as much detail as you can about these individuals. Keep the information *encrypted* in your computer and keep a backup copy off site. (Be cautious: Political troublemaker Jim Bell was sentenced to a long prison term for doing little more than this; officials felt "threatened" by it because of his attitude and history as the author of the essay "Assasination Politics.")

- Take a walk around your neighborhood and think about how you'd defend it if you had to. Later, take steps to acquire any needed supplies or have any pertinent discussions with neighbors about our potentially dangerous future. (Be careful not to "conspire" unless you're sure everyone you're talking with is both honest and discreet.)

- *Unofficially* seize… expropriate… confiscate… whatever you want to call it… the property of those who unjustly but *officially* seize property in your city.

- Like Robin Hood, give some seized item *back* to a person whose property was stolen. Do it anonymously; your heart will love it.

- Send money to an arrested person's legal defense fund.

- Destroy seized property before the government can get its ill-gotten profit from it (but only after you're sure the victim has no chance of getting it back).

- Ostracize those who buy unconstitutionally seized property. Educate others about why they should not help government agencies loot the innocent.
- Call the Fully Informed Jury Association and learn what you can do to help. 1-800-TEL-JURY.
- Organize siege teams that can be dispatched to observe, report on, and possibly help prevent government assaults.

Finally, and above all, remember that rage can be useful, even necessary in its proper time and place. Don't lose a bit of your fury. But bank it for the future. Save it for that rainy day. And remember Thomas Paine's words (on pages 84 and 85). The struggle for freedom *is* hard — and one of the hardest parts may be waiting and wondering when the right time will come (or to fear that the right time may already be here and nobody is acting).

The main thing to remember: When you act, do more harm to tyrants than they do to us.

I mean, to me the way you tell the good guys from the bad guys is... the good guys don't want nothing of yours and don't care what you do with what you got. The bad guys, on the other hand, want to know where you got what you got; want to know where their cut of what you got... is. They want to know what you're going to do with what you got... and then they want to try to impress you enough... so that you'll invest what you got left, after they got what you got, in something that they got. And that's so you high school dropouts can understand what's happening here. — Clayton R. Douglas, publisher of *The Free American*, January 20, 1998

37. Are smart cards a smart idea?

Many of us tend to have a knee-jerk reaction against "the cashless society." And rightly so. The systems now being put in place by banks and governments impose upon us devices that will track our spending, and therefore our movements and our habits. These intrusions are obnoxious, and let's pity the fools who buy the claims of "convenience!" and "security!" being used to sell them.

The smart card is being pushed as (among other things) a substitute for your ATM card — and eventually your checkbook, drivers license, insurance ID, etc. It's simply a plastic card, like all those others, but with a microchip on it that's capable of storing a stunning — and potentially very dangerous — amount of data. One thing it's capable of storing is money, in electronic form. Thus its role in the spooky "cashless society."

But don't dismiss the so-called "smart card" out of hand. In certain manifestations, it could be a fine tool for freedom. Yes, *all* electronically readable cards that tie into central databases, keyed to your name and ID Number, are to be avoided. But take the same card, buy it *anonymously* in a store, pre-charged with the amount of money of your choice, and activated by an *anonymously-issued* PIN number, and you have a very handy little gadget, just like the phone cards you can now get everywhere. These aren't available yet. But watch for them in the not-too-distant future.

You can use such a card almost as anonymously as cash, but without the temptations cash presents — either to freelance thieves or the thieves who now work as bagmen for various forfeiture-rich government agencies. Your security would be breached only if an agency took the partially-used card from you and got a record of your purchases. If you used the card up, then destroyed it, no one would ever know you'd had it — just like a store-bought phone card. Otherwise, you could use it with true convenience and security.

The government will no doubt try to ban, or regulate, this type of card, so be careful of that. But so far, they haven't done it to phone cards, so maybe they won't see these free-market smart cards on their paranoia radar screens for a while, either.

> *"The bank is something else than men. It happens that every man in a bank hates what the bank does, and yet the bank does it. The bank is something more than men, I tell you. It's the monster. Men made it, but they can't control it."* — John Steinbeck, *The Grapes of Wrath*

38. What about those damn fingerprints at the bank?

Increasingly, banks are now requiring fingerprints from non-customers who cash checks drawn on customers' accounts. This is, of course, just one more of many outrages. Banks are right up there with their co-conspirator governments when it comes to treating human beings like trash.

This is one more reason for getting away from banks altogether. But realistically, that isn't doable in all circumstances. Unless everyone who ever pays you money is willing to do it in cash or postal money orders (something we should all encourage), banks are a reality in your life.

What can you do? Well, here are some ideas, with varying degrees of risk or confrontation:

- Go to the drive-up window instead of the inside teller. If they pass the print pad out to your car (which some do), have somebody else — anybody else — in the vehicle with you, and use *their* thumb instead of yours. Maybe you can offer your thumb as a substitute for theirs sometime. Unfortunately, some banks will require you to go inside to give a print, so this won't always work.

- A more principled, but more dangerous, approach is to remind the bank that the funds don't belong to them, but to the person who gave you the check, and that if the bank is refusing to release the funds once you've identified yourself, they're violating a contract with their own customer. There are two problems with this approach. One is that, while it's philosophically correct, it may not be true in a practical sense to say that a bank has this type of contract with its customer. Banks impose all kinds of unilateral "agreements" on their customers, and the fedgov imposes all sorts of arcane rules on banks that overrule decent, ethical relationships. Legally, the money your friend deposited in the bank belongs... yeah, *to the bank*! The second difficulty is that I've heard several accounts of people being "escorted" from banks, or even arrested, when pressing this point. It's not for the shy.

- You can, however, sue the person who gave you the check, claiming bad faith and breach of contract. Again, hard to say where such a suit might go, but it could be interesting if the person you're suing is in sympathy with you and aids you in this suit as a test case against the bank's policies.

- Ask, with extreme innocence in your demeanor, what crime they suspect you of committing. Act puzzled and hurt. Embarrass bank personnel and slow up the works while not getting loud or intimidating. (This approach probably works best for women and old people.)

- Deface your fingerprints in some temporary or permanent way before dealing with the bank. With old, nondigitized methods of reading fingerprints, it used to be quite easy to temporarily deface prints enough to make them unreadable. A brushing with sandpaper would do it, as would a spate of hard work that roughened up the prints, or the use of some harsh, common chemicals. Many women (particularly of Asian extraction) have such light prints, naturally, that their patterns can scarcely be read. Digitized methods do a much better job of detecting patterns, however, experienced readers have written to suggest such things as a light coat of plastic on the thumb or a coating of canola oil.

Twentieth-century man believes in the state as firmly and implicitly as medieval man believed in the church — as an institution whose authority can't, finally, be questioned. I don't mean that people never complain about the government; obviously they complain about it all the time. But they very rarely challenge it in principle by asking where it gets its right to exist in the first place. More often than not, even their complaints are really demands that it do more than it is already doing. — Joseph Sobran, *Arizona Republic*, December 14, 1990

39. The Declaration of Disobedience

Maybe this will help motivate you toward your freedom goals. It's the work of correspondent Carl Alexander, who invites you to modify it to fit your own beliefs and objectives. I had nothing to do with writing it, but I'm proud that something I wrote inspired Carl to create it. I think sections III and IV are particularly outstanding as guides to personal ethics and conduct.

DECLARATION OF DISOBEDIENCE

WHEREAS: The Federal Government is in flagrant & repeated violation of the Constitution of the United States of America, its unique political contract with The People of the United States of America, and;

WHEREAS: The State and Local Governments act in collusion with, or by coercion from, said Federal Government, also resulting in flagrant & repeated violations of their political contracts with The People, and;

WHEREAS: This state of affairs pertaining, does afflict and intrude upon the God-given Unalienable Rights of The People, and upon the established Constitutional guarantees set forth in the Bill of Rights, and causes them great harm and suffering:

THEREFORE, BE IT KNOWN, that I _____, a citizen of the United States of America, do hereby declare & affirm the following, from this day forward, until such time as my Proper and Just Rights as an American citizen are restored:

Section I. Breach of Contract.

A. I hereby declare null & void the previously existing Political Contract between myself, and the Federal Government of the United States of America, and all of its agencies, branches, bureaus, commissions, departments, agents, employees, officials, and representatives.

B. I hereby withdraw my sanction and consent from the Federal Government, and from any entity acting upon its behalf or at its behest, and do declare all statements made and all actions taken by such entities, in my name as a citizen, to be null & void.

C. Until such time as lawful and constitutional government is restored to the United States of America, I hereby reserve & retain my right to appoint or elect any others to serve in my stead, and will hereafter & do now, represent myself in all commercial, legal, political, social, and international affairs.

Section II. Actionable Behavior.

A. This Declaration of Disobedience is duly based upon the illegitimate and unconstitutional actions of the Federal Government of the United States of America, repeatedly made and invariably pursued, towards usurpation of the legitimate and proper rights of the Citizenry.

B. In partial proof of this repeated train of abuses, let the following facts of surreptitious laws enacted, during a single Congressional Session, be submitted to whom it may concern:

1. Public Law 104-193: Establishes a National database of all employed persons. Violation of the Fourth Amendment. 2. Public Law 104-191: Establishes "Health Care Crimes" and permits seizure of assets from Doctors & patients. Violation of Fourth, Fifth, Sixth, & Seventh Amendments. 3. Public Law 104-191: Permits seizure of assets from any person establishing a foreign citizenship. Violation of Fourth, Ninth & Tenth Amendments. 4. Public Law 104-191: Establishes government access to all health records of citizens, including statements made by patients to doctors. Violation of First, Fourth, Fifth, Ninth & Tenth Amendments. 5. Public Law 104-208: Makes it a federal crime to keep or bear arms within any local "school zone." Establishes misdemeanors as basis for denial of Constitutional guarantees. Violation of Second, Fourth, Ninth & Tenth Amendments. 6. Public Law 104-132: Establishes "Star Chamber" Courts & secret trials. Allows citizens to be designated as "terrorists," held without bail or charges in secret locations, & have unsubstantiated secret testimony used against them. Violation of Fourth, Fifth, Sixth, and Eighth Amendments. 7. Public Law 104-208: Mandates "de facto" National Identification Cards for all citizens, and establishes mandatory finger-

printing of all citizens[2], as well as a coded & secret database on all citizens. Violation of Fourth, Ninth & Tenth Amendments.

Section III. Personal Sanctions.

A. I will no longer obey any law, rule or regulation which is not in clear accordance with the provisions of the Constitution of the United States of America, as commonly understood in the plain English language.

B. I shall resist the enforcement of any law, rule or regulation upon my person, property, or life which is not in clear accordance with the provisions of the aforesaid Political Contract.

C. All forms of duties, fees, levies, and taxes hereafter paid in my name to the Federal Government, or its agents, are rendered under protest, and considered taken by duress, under threat of force.

Section IV. Personal Conduct.

A. Until such time as lawful and constitutional government is again restored to the United States of America, and in pursuance thereof, I will hereby alter my normal behavior as a sovereign American citizen, in the following manner:

1. I will no longer exercise my franchise to vote for federal elected "representatives," or on any federal question or issue.

2. I will no longer petition, or otherwise interact with, any "representative" of federal government, as a constituent.

3. I will no longer demonstrate respect towards any official or high office of federal government, without good cause.

4. I will no longer accede authority to, cooperate with, or be courteous to any government bureaucrat, without good cause.

5. I will no longer avail myself of federal programs, services, or "benefits."

---

[2] The law mandates unspecified "security features." These may include fingerprints, retinal scans, digitized photographs (possibly incorporating facial recognition), iris scans, DNA codes, etc. As of this writing, the details are unknown.

6. I will no longer work for, contract with, sell to, support, or otherwise aid federal government.

7. I will no longer purchase goods or merchandise of new manufacture, which provides government with higher amounts of tax revenue.

8. I will no longer fly the Flag of the United States of America, but instead substitute the Gadsden Flag DON'T TREAD ON ME!

9. I will no longer consider any government capable of, or willing, to protect my person or my Just Rights. I will keep and bear arms.

10. I will no longer take my Constitutional Rights for granted, but will jealously guard and vigorously exercise them all.

11. I will no longer treat my fellow American citizens as strangers, but as my friends and as my neighbors. I will help them to understand and exercise their rights as American citizens.

12. I will no longer live my life without the Liberty which is my birthright as an American citizen.
Section V. Affirmation.

With renewed reliance on the protection of Divine Providence, and with firm resolve, I do solemnly swear or attest that the above Declaration is a true and accurate statement of my beliefs, and intentions, So Help Me God.

_____ (Signature)
_____ (Date)
_____ (Witness)
_____ (Witness)

If you are living in one of those countries where freedom has been lost and you want to fight to get it back, you have to expect you are going to be in the minority. Most of your friends and neighbors aren't going to want to join you. In fact, most of them will

---

gladly turn you in just so they can earn a little credit with the local boss. If you succeed in winning freedom back, they won't give a damn, they won't thank you, and they will probably hate your guts for taking away the goodies the local tyrant was handing out as rewards for people who would rather be comfortable than free.

DON'T SACRIFICE YOURSELF TO WIN FREE-DOM FOR SOMEBODY ELSE. — Jefferson Mack, *Secret Freedom Fighter*

40. Shrug

Ayn Rand said it better than anybody could. Shrug. Don't give the benefit of your abilities to a society that abuses and rejects everything you value. Shrug. Perform menial work, or spend only a few hours a week selling your real abilities in support of a corrupt system. Live for freedom, not for those who take freedom away.

It is not necessary to imagine the world ending in fire or ice. There are two other possibilities: One is paperwork, and the other is nostalgia. — Frank Zappa

41. Some spare Social Security numbers

Here are some Social Security numbers nobody's using at the moment. Now, of course, you wouldn't get away with it if you tried to use these in any instance where someone actually might *check*. But if someone's just being snoopy and you'd rather gum up their snoop works than have a confrontation by refusing to show your SS tattoo, I assure you none of the following folks will care if you "borrow" their numbers:

River Phoenix, dead vegetarian — 571-61-9058

Richard Nixon, dead con artist — 567-68-0515

Gary Gilmore, dead publicity hound — 143-32-5892

James Morrison, dead (or alive?) rock star — 190-32-1736

Elvis Presley, definitely dead rock star — 409-52-2002

Vito Genovese, dead private-sector gangster — 145-24-5159

Lyndon Baines Johnson, dead public-sector gangster — 577-60-6128

Nelson Aldrich Rockefeller, dead Illuminatus — 056-09-0954

Jack Kerouac, like, dead, man — 022-14-5342

Maria von Trapp, dead nanny — 009-32-2317

Timothy Leary, dead exopsychologist — 032-07-5410

Thurman Munson, dead baseball player — 289-46-5337

Leroy "Satchel" Paige, dead philosopher — 497-14-0755

Agnes Belushi, dead mother of dead actor — 289-16-8450

Billy Carter, dead brother of living dead president — 410-52-0294

J. Edgar Hoover, dead crossdresser — 577-60-1114

Clyde Tolson, dead Very Good Friend of J. Edgar Hoover — 577-60-2204

Paul Robeson, dead singing communist — 071-12-7669

Audie Murphy, dead Texan — 459-28-6632

Karen Silkwood, dead accident victim — 456-78-0131

Wladzui "Walter" Valentino Liberace, dead famously famous person — 472-14-4916

Harland Sanders, dead cholesterol pusher — 237-34-7258

Cass Elliot, dead fat lady who sang — 228-52-8238

If none of these defunct celebrities appeal to you, you'll find Social Security numbers of 50 million more famous, infamous and non-famous dead people in the Social Security Death Index (www.ancestry.com/search/retype/vital/ssdi/main.htm). That's where most, though not all, the above info came from. The index contains information only on people whose estates applied to the federal government for the lump-sum death benefit they were "entitled" to. (Nelson Rockefeller — can you believe it!) You won't find many hoity toity folks like Jacqueline Kennedy Onassis. But you'll find plenty to keep you morbidly busy for hours.

Here's a colorful little sidelight: According to the record, that famous government lover, Lyndon B. Johnson, didn't bother to get a Social Security number until he was vice president of the U.S. Of course, as a Senator he was above and beyond the laws that govern mere humans. (Congress exempted itself from socialist insecurity.) But even before he joined the elite, it appears he never bought that line we were handed about how you have to have a number in order to work. "J. Hoover," as the database calls him, also didn't get a Social Security number until after 1960. Interesting attitudes these guys had...

When you discover you are riding a dead horse, the best strategy is to dismount. — Dakota Sioux saying

42. Consider the Sovereign Society

The Sovereign Society, created in 1998, offers offshore financial benefits to members for a modest membership fee. This isn't for the poorest of the poor. But you don't have to be the richest of the rich, either. With membership at $195 U.S. per year, a person of middle-class means, with a serious commitment to financial privacy, could take great advantage of this service:

The Sovereign Society
5 Catherine Street
Waterford, Ireland
voice: + (353) 51-844-068
U.S. toll-free (888) 358-8125
fax: + (353) 51-304-561
e-mail: info@thesovereignsociety.com
www.sovereignsociety.com

The Sovereign Society is the creation of Bob Kephart and Bill Bonner (owners of Scope International) and is supported by such figures as Lord William Rees-Mogg, Douglas Casey and Vince Miller (International Society for Individual Liberty). It offers members a variety of benefits, including:

- Your choice of three European bank accounts with moderate minimum entry requirements (though quite high requirements for many services). The accounts remain "dry" until you activate them with your first deposit.

- The book *The Whole World Catalog* (offshore products and services);

- Several freedom-oriented newsletters and reports;

- The services of JML Swiss Investment Counseling;
- Mail and fax forwarding services.

We are ready for an unforeseen event that may or may not occur. — Dan Quayle

43. Wear garlic to your next IRS audit

If you've gotta go to an audit, go with all the proper security safeguards. Some experts recommend tape recorders (one on the table, one hidden in your pocket or purse in case the fedgov snags the first one) and witnesses. I, not being hampered by expertise in anything, recommend garlic.

Oh, there's nothing wrong with the tapes and witnesses. Good ideas, in fact! But a necklace of garlic cloves can't do any harm, either. And given the sort of creatures you run into at IRS offices, garlic jewelry could just save you from spending the rest of your life wearing lead sunglasses and sleeping all day in a coffin lined with your native soil.

Besides, if the auditor isn't bright enough to understand the Dracula movie symbolism, it will be totally distracted by the sheer oddity of your appearance. And if it is bright enough to understand the message you're sending, it will be distracted for other reasons. If you're lucky (not likely) it might even be distracted by giggles.

I dare you.

But seriously now, folks...

The first day they take your freedom away, they are only too happy to let you get up in the morning, eat breakfast with the kids, take off for the office or the factory, and put in a full day's work. It's only when you have gotten used to their being around that they start cracking down, taking a little piece at a time, a day at a time. Every inch of the way they will keep tell-

ing you it's all for your own good and safety. That's bullshit. The only reason political leaders take freedom away is for their own good and safety. That's the way they make sure they keep their jobs. — Jefferson Mack, *Secret Freedom Fighter*

44. Tape it!

Since we are dealing with "authorities" who can be so paranoid, so mean, and so utterly unprincipled — and get away with it — let's do all we can to protect ourselves.

One way is to do our best to tape every encounter with any official who might be able or inclined to deny us our rights or otherwise harm us. Sometimes this will mean whipping out your video camera, as with those nice people who made Indiana's Lt. King so nervous, back in Item 26. But that's not always possible. A microcassette tape recorder, however, can be kept handy in pocket, purse, car console or backpack for instant recording of most encounters.

Microcassette recorders are inexpensive (under $30), operate quietly, use easily available power supplies (AA batteries) and can be activated with a press of a thumb or sometimes by voice. For optimal recording you should use a plug-in microphone instead of relying on the mike built into the machine. The built-in mike isn't great quality, anyway, and if you're trying to use it through layers of clothing or from the bottom of your fanny pack, you might end up with little on your tape but the sounds of rustling fabric. These mikes also have the irritating habit of recording the sounds of the tape spinning and the motor running. A simple little lapel mike from Radio Shack should do the trick nicely. In a purse or fanny pack, you can just clip it somewhere near the top, then keep the bag open. You could wear it brazenly, clipped to a pocket or collar, but in most cases you probably won't want the government person, banker or other freedom-obstructionist to know she's being recorded. In that case, you could clip it inside a pocket, hide it under a scarf, decorative pin or corsage, or inside a pocket protector. (Unless you keep the recorder in the same pocket — not always feasible — you'll need to find a way to run the wire under your clothing, as well.)

Whether taped evidence can be used in court, and how it can be used there, depends on state law. You also need to be aware of your state's law on making any secret tape, for any purpose, of a conversation in which you're participating. It is against federal law to intercept a conversation in which you aren't participating — unless you have a warrant or are a privileged fed. But in a situation where it's you against them, particularly when the "them" in question is likely to be given more credibility than you (like a cop or banker), a tape could be a handy item to have.

> *Comes a time in every man's life when he spits on his hands, hoists the black flag, and commences to cutting throats.* — H.L. Mencken

45. An Inspirational example: Operation Sink Kyl

There are people in the world who just have a natural *élan* when it comes to messing with the heads of politicians. One of those is the mysterious Miguel Cartero of Arizona. His Gun Owners Liberation Front, GOLF (for people teed-off at government excess) made several witty assaults on the dignity of politicians during the crucial election seasons of the mid-nineties.

Perhaps the most brilliant GOLF game — one you can easily emulate — was the organization's very first effort, launched at the height of election season 1994 and aimed at "Clinton Republican," Jon Kyl (now Senator Jon Kyl). What was actually aimed symbolically at Kyl during this campaign was...well, there's just no genteel way to say it...urine. Here's how Cartero & Company put it in their e-mail announcement of the Sink Kyl campaign:

> Are you pissed off about the recently passed Crime Bill? Do you feel a dam of frustration about to burst every time you think about what Congress has done to you? Does the mere thought of Clinton Republicans give you a burning sensation? Well, help is on the way.
>
> Here is just the thing to get your juices flowing again. Just what you need to relieve the pressure building up inside of you. It's your gift from the Whiz Kids at the Gun Owners Liberation Front. It's yours and it's free — because we aim to please.
>
> Attached is your very own, copier-ready artwork for the new, splash-hit Jon Kyl urinal target. Simply run off as many copies as you like for yourself and all your similarly frustrated friends.
>
> Once you have made as many copies as you think you'll need, it's a good idea to laminate them. That way they'll be plastic-coated, just like the original. To do this, all you need is a spray can of clear urethane (available for about $3 from Ace Hardware). Simply coat both sides real well, wait for them to dry, and then cut out the individual targets from the sheets. Now you're ready to put Jon in his place (Why do you think they named it after him?) and finally get some relief.

Attached to the message was a handsome graphic of Mr. Kyl, suitable for re-printing six-up on a standard piece of office paper, which GOLF members proceeded to print out, waterproof and attach to urinals all over Arizona. Oh, to "test the effectiveness of the campaign," Supreme Commander

Cartero asked each targeteer to mail one target back to GOLF with an account of how many they'd made and distributed. One little thing: the address given for GOLF was actually that of Jon Kyl campaign headquarters. Don't you just love a mind that works like that?

> *The United States is a nation of laws: badly written and randomly enforced.* — Frank Zappa

46. Hobbit and Parker talk guns

101 Things To Do 'Til the Revolution included a section on guns. People who like firearms are an opinionated bunch, so I admitted my limitations, then ducked to await the onslaught of disagreement.

To my surprise, just two had a lot to say about that part of the book. One was Hobbit, a lawyer from Oregon, who knows guns because in addition to teaching about and shooting them, he sometimes sells them. The other was Parker, an old buddy from Dampest Washington, who knows guns because he likes to slaughter cute, helpless, furry little animals.[3]

Both wrote to say, "You're a girl! What do you know?" So when it came time to write the gun section in this book...well, I thought I'd let *them* take the heat, instead of me. I asked Hobbit and Parker a few questions, and didn't let them see each other's answers until after they'd both been put on the spot, individually. Here's what they came up with:

---

[3] "And," he adds, "hang their limp and lifeless carcasses from my walls."

Hobbit and Parker speak

1. *A gang of strangers in black face masks is kicking down your door at 4:00 a.m., screaming something you can't understand. What firearm do you want to have at your bedside, and why?*

Hobbit: I want a GAU-30 on a pintle mount. That's the Gatling gun clone used in the A-10 aircraft for tank busting. There's no body armor in the world going to stop 30-mm armor-piercing depleted uranium rounds at 10,000 rounds per minute. Or their cute little armored personnel carrier outside, either.

The problem with this question is that if I expect people are going to be kicking in my door at 4:00 a.m., then I arrange to be somewhere else. If I can't leave, then I would opt for a .30 caliber battle rifle (M1-A, FN-FAL, HK91) with magazines full of armor piercing ammunition. However — I do not generally expect the boys in black to be kicking in my door, so what I would end up meeting them with is what I would normally have by the bedside — a 12-gauge Remington 870 loaded with 0 buck. Seeing the body armor, I would shoot for pelvises and legs instead of chests.

Parker: What I want most is to be elsewhere. If I can't have that, I want a .50 caliber machine gun, because there's a lot of them and only one of me, and I'd much rather patch up some half inch holes in my living room than have the new owners of my house repainting the bedroom where I died.

However, I think I'd take a 12-gauge shotgun and hide or run. Obviously, my chances would be better if I'd planned for this contingency beforehand, and built an escape hatch of some kind. Your firearm is only one ingredient of your midnight survival package, but if you have to use it, somebody, somewhere is going to make some after-the-fact decisions concerning your actions.

Why a shotgun? Rifles and some handguns have a problem with over-penetration in a residential setting. Their bullets may go through walls and harm innocent people on the other side. Shotguns are my home defense favorite, within the limitations of their practical accuracy. I like pump-action shotguns, which require two hands for reliable operation. Do your homework with different loads in your particular gun. For example, at 20-30 feet, many shot loads will still be a solid mass of lead, so don't shoot between two assailants hoping to wing them both.

2. *Your resistance unit is in the woods fighting soldiers wearing blue helmets. What's the number-one firearm you want to have in your hands?*[4]

Hobbit: Whatever the soldiers are carrying. Each of them then becomes a potential source of resupply.

Parker: Tactically, the expedient move would be to kill an opponent and take whatever he had, which would likely be an M16 if the invading troops were NATO, or an AK47 variation if they were "other." Problem is, I personally don't care for either of these rifles or their cartridges, preferring instead the older military designs. So what, you say? Right. Choose your personal small arm in .223 or 7.62x39, and you'll be one up on me.

If you are prepared to take things off of dead soldiers, don't limit yourself to their guns and ammo. Certainly you and your buddies can find uses for radios, explosives and

---

[4] See Item 61 for a contrary opinion on this question.

body armor, and maybe even vehicles or crew-served weapons. If you don't take these, at least render them unusable by the enemy.

3. *You have been driven into the woods and forced to survive by hunting. There is a variety of game available, from quail to bear. You have just one firearm. What is it?*

Parker: Forced? Forced??? How, for God's sake? Tell me!

Seriously...My kind of question. First of all, if you're going to survive *solely* by hunting, get used to being hungry. There are other hunters out there, two-legged and four-legged, and some of them are much more skilled than you. It won't be long before you've hunted out your territory, and then what? If, on the other hand, you are hunting to supplement your otherwise meager diet (or that of your family), you can do okay.

What are you hunting for? In my humble opinion, small game is best since there's a lot more of it, and you can make good use of the smaller packages without refrigeration. You want a low-power round that won't rip up a lot of meat, which means .22 or 20-gauge to me. There are combination guns (the Savage model 24 being a good example) that mount a rifle barrel over a shotgun barrel, in several different chamberings. I find the .30-30 over 20-gauge most appealing. Many meat hunters use rifles, with bolt and lever actions being the most common.

If you are being forced to survive by hunting, chances are good that when you kill some grocery item, you don't want to attract the attention of someone who will take it away from you (or you away from it). If you want to hunt quietly, check out archery, including crossbows. Plan to practice a lot, though, or gain a new appreciation of the word "hunger".

Hobbit: This seems to presume that whoever drove me there is going to leave me alone. I'd probably go for one of the "over/under" rifle-shotgun combinations, say the Stevens 24C Camper (.22LR barrel over a 20-gauge shotgun). Or possibly, if allowed by the rules, a Thompson Contender with three or four different barrels.

An interesting argument could also be made for a scoped and suppressed .22 semiautomatic. A .22 is not the best first choice for larger game, but placed properly it will bring down most anything I'd care to shoot. The suppressor makes it unlikely to attract any attention, a big plus considering that "driven" verb.

4. *You have only one gun, which you must use for every, single, possible purpose. It's all you can afford. What is it?*[5]

Parker: It's a travesty of justice, a crying shame, and a disappointment of epic proportions. It's a big mistake, it may be your death warrant, and at the very least you won't be sleeping well at night, 'cause you're only one gun away from no guns at all.

It means you have no spare, if your one gun is disabled or taken from you. It means if your very bestest friend in the whole world is in imminent danger, you can't give him a gun without disarming yourself. It means that you'll be performing one or more gun-related functions poorly, or perhaps not at all.

---

[5] Firearms guru Michael Harries (Item 61) objected to this question when I showed him what I had asked Hobbit and Parker. I should point out that I also object; it's folly to have just one firearm for all purposes. I included the question because others say that *some people* will, because of lack of budget, lack of interest, or whatever, only own one firearm. I'm with Parker. If you can afford just one gun, hock your TV set or your four-wheeler.

Please, take another job. Sell a couple of chickens. Split firewood for your neighbor until your hands are sore and bleeding. Sit down for a heart to heart talk with your rich uncle (remind him Christmas is coming). Do what-the-hell-ever it takes to obtain at least one more gun.

We may meet sometime, when I have only one gun on or about my person (don't count on it, but it could happen). But to only own one gun? There's no excuse for that.

Hobbit: Smith and Wesson 686, 4-inch barrel. It's reasonably concealable, will handle most game I'd hunt with a handgun, and has more than enough power for self defense purposes, but can be loaded with .38 Special ammunition for inexpensive practice. Built like a tank, it will outlast me.

5. *You are a 125-pound woman whose car has died on a lonely road. Another motorist stops, but as he approaches you, a crawly feeling tells you he's not here to help. Your hand slowly creeps down toward a gun wedged beside the seat. What is it and what's it loaded with?*

Parker: Hmmm. Never done this before. Does my hair look okay?....Wherever your gun is, let go of it and roll up the window. Lock the damn door. Tell him you're having car problems and ask him to call a tow truck. Regardless of your crawly feeling a gun is not a good first answer to this question. Anyway, you should hold it under your jacket until you really need it.

Self-defense guns are possibly the biggest argument-starter in the entire gun universe. Fortunately, gun owners are frequently armed, so the arguments are almost always polite, but seldom have more words been expended in a more useless cause.

I have three requirements for carrying guns. First, they must be light and compact enough that you will carry them all the time. Second, you must be able to shoot them well, and instinctively, which means lots of practice. Third, they must be sufficiently powerful to perform the self defense function, which most people agree to mean not less than a .38 Special for revolvers or 9mm (maaaayyyybe .380) in autoloaders.

Many 125-pound women, once they become familiar with it, can handle the recoil of a short .38 Special revolver without undue strain.[6] These are simple to load and operate, good ones are less finicky about different types of ammo and somewhat less expensive on today's market than comparable quality autos, and the ladies who pack them don't often feel the need for more than five or six rounds. The ammo is probably some medium to hot load of jacketed hollow point, as most criminal confrontations are sudden, up-close, and what your boss would call "time-critical." JHP's (jacketed hollow points) expand on impact and do the maximum damage when you need it.

Much more important is the one iron-clad requirement I have for people who carry guns. It is absolutely *imperative* that you think out the moral ramifications of using deadly force in the unhurried comfort of your own mind, and decide for certain whether you could kill an attacker if it was a choice of you or him. The moment of truth is no time to agonize over this question; the slimeball will sense

---

[6] This is another area in which I'll vehemently disagree with my sexist friends. Most 125-pound women, given average arm- and upper-body strength and the right attitude, can handle just about any handgun. I know; I'm one of those 125-pound women. In my totally stubborn opinion, a .38 is *too puny*. There are some nice, compact .45 ACP autoloaders and .357 revolvers on the market that make very good carry guns.

your hesitation, take away your gun and kill you with it. Now, we not only have to comfort your grieving relatives, but also those of the victims he murdered with your gun. Forget the rest of my opinions, but remember this: PRACTICE THIS ATTITUDE AT HOME BEFORE YOU TAKE IT OUT IN PUBLIC! Please.

Hobbit: Presuming that a gun — and not a cellular call to a towing service — is the solution to the problem, the gun's in the wrong darned place, for starters. Picture this — gun is wedged in seat. A common means of car attacks start with hitting your car from behind. The FBI in a famous Miami shootout disaster found out that that quickly puts your gun on the floorboard — and you DON'T need to be grabbing around on the floor, in the dark, looking for your gun while the Forces of Evil are closing in. That's Darwin Award City, there.

Gun in handbag is no better. Holster. On belt. Attached to you. They make special driving holsters, should you so require.

Back to the primary question... With proper training and attitude, it doesn't matter what the woman is carrying — she's most likely going to win. If she's a leaf-eating herbivore who just happened to notice this ugly disgusting gun in her rental car and was on her way to the police station to turn it in — she's goblin bait.

Let's presume the first, though, and although the size is a bit large we can just offer what my wife carries — a Smith and Wesson Model 66, 2½" barrel loaded with hot .38 Special +P cartridges. If she would practice just a bit more I'd graduate her over to, oh, say an S&W 3913 9mm. Shuffle guns (semi-automatics) need a bit more attention than roller guns (revolvers), though, and she doesn't want to spend quite that much time.

6. *Now, what else do you want to say?*

Hobbit: Before making any decision regarding firearms, you should go back to basics. First, the purpose of a weapon is to convince someone or something to change its course of action. Firearms are tools used as weapons, and their application in that role is as precise as that of any other tool. Nothing mystical or magical about it, but just as you wouldn't use a hammer to cut a board, certain guns may be more or less suited for the task at hand.

Secondly, and somewhat tangentially, I've always been convinced that problems are best solved while small — or even avoided altogether when possible. Just because I carry a spare tire in the car doesn't mean that I want to use it. Likewise with firearms, just having them doesn't mean I plan to use them (not being a Bambi killer). But as with the spare tire, they would be a comfort should they be needed.

And I should make sure I know how and when to use them, not try to figure it out on the fly. Which brings us to:

Finally, one basic difficulty in answering these questions was, "What level of skill does the question presume?" The hardened hunter/shooter/military veteran? The novice who barely knows where the safety is? Or someone in between? In connection with this is the question of attitude — is the person willing to use the firearm as it needs to be used?

Claire said we were to keep this short, but these final comments alone fill up whole books and weeks' long training courses. Let me summarize by saying that good training and poor guns is far better than poor training and good guns. Having the best tool for the job and being afraid to pull the trigger is far worse than having the most miserable Saturday Night Special conceivable — but with full intent to shoot straight and make each shot count.

Parker: Nothing we have to say will make you buy guns you don't like, or keep you from buying the ones you want. After all, we're not going to change *our* gun-buying habits to fit *your* preferences. The fact that you're an armed American is good enough for us.

Guns are tools. They are designed to do a certain task, just like a saw is made for cutting wood, and a toothbrush is made to scrub your teeth. The particular task of a gun is often surrounded by a bunch of emotional baggage, but it amounts to this: what we expect from a gun (and its ammunition) is to store a specified amount of chemical energy until a specified time, and then expend that energy by propelling a small object in a specific direction fast enough to damage or destroy things. Who, what, when, where, and why are subject to human interpretation, but the basic function remains the same.

Just like cars, different guns have different specifications. You might like to drive a Formula One racer/Peterbilt dump truck/'32 Ford 5-window coupe, but it's not the ideal vehicle for commuting to work and picking up the groceries. All of these are customized to perform a certain function, and so it is with guns. If you need to shoot through an engine block, don't expect to kill squirrels for supper with the same gun, and vice versa. This is why someone might own dozens, or perhaps hundreds, of firearms — because different guns do different things (or at least, do the same things differently).

So let's think of some broad uses that a firearm may be put to. Hunting, competitive target shooting, military combat, historic display, self defense; each one of these has many variations, and there are others.

When you're getting accustomed to handling guns, you should shoot at least 100 rounds a week. That makes a .22 a good first choice. A .22 is easy to shoot, ammo is cheap, and you won't have to wrestle with it to hit what you aim at. Also, just about every gun owner has one or more .22s, so you can almost always scare up a partner for a weekend plinking session.

If you are not familiar with guns, the best way to learn is to hang around with those who are. Ask them questions, shoot with them, listen to them B.S. together over a beverage. Shooters, by and large, are friendly folks. They enjoy their hobby, and they are willing to share their knowledge with novices, especially novices who don't get in the way and keep their muzzles pointed in a safe direction. They will probably let you shoot their favorite guns. Don't drop their guns in the mud or perforate the truck fenders, okay? It is a good thing to shoot as many different guns as you can get your hands on, just for the experience.

When you meet another responsible gun owner, the two of you have something in common that people who don't own guns cannot easily understand. You are essentially saying, "I am armed, and I respect your right to be as well. We are equals in a very basic sense, because each of us could kill the other, but for our personal discipline and restraint. I trust you with arms." Though you may disagree on other matters, you each have decided to bear directly the burden of your personal survival, and that can be the basis for a degree of mutual respect.

A hand from Washington will be stretched out and placed upon every man's business; the eye of the federal inspector will be in every man's counting house... The law will of necessity have inquisical features, it will provide penalties, it will create complicated machinery. Under it, men will be hauled into courts distant from their homes. Heavy fines imposed by distant and unfamiliar tribunals will constantly menace the taxpayer. An army of federal inspectors, spies, and detectives will descend upon the state. — Virginia House Speaker Richard E. Byrd, 1910, predicting what would happen if a federal income tax became law.

47. Learn to use those guns!

You can find an extensive list of local and national shooting schools, including their addresses, phone numbers, and Web sites (if they have them) at:

www.martialartsresource.com/firearms.htm

Some of the most well-reputed schools include:

Gunsite (Arizona): www.gunsite.net/

InSights Training Center (Washington state): www.insightstraining.com/

Lethal Force Institute (New Hampshire): www.ayoob.com/

Thunder Ranch (Texas): www.thunderranchinc.com/

Front Sight (California and Nevada): www.frontsight.com/

While most schools that teach heavy-duty techniques admit non-government employees as well as government agents, some have an incredibly snotty attitude toward the people they call "civilians" (as if police weren't civilians —

which they indeed are). One even requires us "civilians" to obtain a permission slip from their local sheriff before being allowed to take its courses — as if we were all criminals until we can prove otherwise. (I'd say those guys have been hanging out with government too long.)

Dr. Ignatius Piazza, founder of Front Sight, is one with a different attitude. He has offered free training to airline pilots and school officials and offers a free one-day course at its Las Vegas facility in shooting submachine guns.

And practice, practice, practice!

Unless you're just mad about firearms or have buckets of money, it's hard to keep in practice. You don't want to go out in rotten weather… can't afford $12.50, $17.50 or more for 50 rounds of ammo… or just… well, there are lots of excuses.

Here are a few things that can help you keep in practice, despite poverty or inertia.

Indoors:

- Unload your gun (And if it's a semi-auto double check that there's no round in the chamber!), then practice dry-firing it in your living room or den. This won't give you the total feel of shooting, of course, but it'll let you practice aiming, shooting from cover, good trigger pull and other skills. If you're concerned about damage to your gun's firing pin from dry-firing, buy some red plastic "snap caps" — inert mock ammo with a spring inside, available at most gun stores — and load your gun with them.

- Purchase a battery-operated indoor target system. You use your regular handgun, but special, battery-powered ammo that sends a signal to an electronic target. (Nothing but the signal exits the barrel; you can use the same ammo over and over.) The target has a "hit" area about three inches across. If your aim is correct, the target flashes red to signal a good shot. These systems sell for as little as $60, which sounds pretty reasonable. However, you'll also need a separate set of battery-powered ammo for each caliber of firearm you shoot, and that can get pricey.

- If you have a pellet gun, you can rig an indoor firing range. Just fill a cardboard box with newspaper or other thick, cushioning material, pin a target to the front of it, and place it in the opening of a fireplace or against some other surface that can take damage without upsetting your significant other, and fire away. At indoor distances, it's highly unlikely you'll ever miss the target. Again, it won't give you the authentic feel of shooting a firearm, but it can help you work on your aim, practice shooting from cover, etc. (Don't try anything *too* athletic, though, like shooting while rolling across the floor. Then you probably *will* miss your target and your housemates will get righteously upset if you punch holes in the sheetrock, the poodle — or them.)

- Take up reloading. While the equipment can be expensive (anywhere from $20 for primitive little hand-held Lee Loader kits to many hundreds for top-of-the-line Dillon progressive reloading presses), reloading can teach you another useful gun-related skill, cut the price of your practice ammo, let you make ammo more accurate than store-bought, and help you maintain your interest in the firearms hobby. (And yes, Parker and Hobbit, even a girl can do it.)

- If you're fortunate enough to have an indoor shooting range available, use it.

Outdoors:

- As Parker says, get a .22. You can buy 500 rounds of ammo for less than the price of 50 rounds of most other ammunition — sometimes for as little as $10 — which is a great help if you're a poor person.

- Commit to some regular, organized shooting activity that relates to the skills you want to practice: silhouette shooting (knocking over steel pigs and chickens); IPSC ("practical shooting") or falling plate for action shooting; trap, skeet, or sporting clays for shotgunning. Even tiny gun clubs usually offer at least one of these activities regularly. While this is no substitute for great self-defense or combat training and practice, anything that helps keep you "in touch" with your firearms and gets you in the habit of shooting can be helpful.

I think the main difference between "us" and "them" is that they have no real sense of humor. And I just think their plans for us peasants are so very funny that "they" just may die laughing. — Michael Harries, firearms instructor

48. "I can't remember!"

My goodness, I just don't know what's the matter with me, these days. I can't even spell my own name correctly. I "forget" things all the time. I can't remember where I've been or to whom I've spoken, or where on earth I hid that handgun of mine. I've suddenly become dyslexic — especially when it comes to putting down numbers on government forms.

Tsk, tsk. Poor me. This is really a problem and no matter how hard I try, it just seems to get worse.

> *Got a complaint about the Internal Revenue Service?*
> *Call the convenient toll-free IRS Taxpayer Complaint*
> *Hot Line number, 1-800-AUDITME.* — Dave Barry

49. Set up your business on the Internet

Even if you can't, or don't want to get yourself out of the U.S.A., you might want to move your business somewhere where it's less likely to be hassled by the American Business Police. Thanks to the Internet, there are a number of ways to do that that don't require that you have a gazillion bucks.

One to check out is Vince Cate's operation on the island of Anguilla:

www.offshore.com.ai/

Vince offers a variety of different services, from a simple Internet account or domain name, to actually helping you locate your computers on the island and sell your products from there. While his full-scale services aren't precisely cheap, he can help you set up an offshore corporation and an account from which to offer it for around $1,500. Not bad, really.

You can also get more information on running an offshore business from Adam Starchild's Cyberhaven:

www.cyberhaven.com

Starchild is the author of *How to Legally Obtain a Second Citizenship and Passport* (Loompanics Unlimited) and *The Offshore Entrepreneur: Profit and Opportunity Have No Borders* (First Street Press). Samples of the latter and related articles are online. Even though some offshore options he talks about do require plenty of money, he's also got tips anyone can use on finding a need and filling it, pitfalls to avoid and so on.

Finally, perhaps the biggest and best offshore site on the Web is EscapeArtist.com (www.escapeartist.com).

For many years, this site has been offering the most comprehensive information on living, banking, and doing business offshore — and not only in the familiar haven countries, but almost anywhere you can think of . From their main page you can go to information on free trade zones, telecommuting from abroad, mail drops, global stock markets, offshore real estate investing and more.

No hype. No slick lawyers trying to sell you overpriced (and under-reliable) offshore investment plans and expensive second passports. Just an unbelievably rich collection of resources from a man, Roger Gallo, who lives the life he writes about and researches.

If you just need basic information on how to set up a business on the Internet, there are quite a few resources — though you'll have to wade through 1) a lot of hype, and 2) outdated information. For starters try:

How to Create Your Own Internet Commerce Business — An online essay by Peter Hand that contains lots of links to useful software and other resources:

www.mcid.com/rmoug99.icpaper.html

And here's a selection of Internet Marketing Books and CDs (though I suggest you read the reader reviews of these same products at Amazon.com before buying):

www.peoplesuccess.com/salnet10.htm

If we were to apply the unmodified, uncurbed, rules of the micro-cosmos (i.e., of the small band or troop, or of, say, our families) to the macro-cosmos (our wider civilization), as our instincts and sentimental yearnings often make us wish to do, we would destroy it. *Yet if we were always to apply the rules of the extended order to our more intimate groupings,* we would crush them. *So we must learn to live in two sorts of worlds at once. To apply the name "society" to both, or even to either, is hardly of any use, and can be most misleading.* — F. A. Hayek

50. The Perpetual Traveler

The Perpetual Traveler (PT) life involves living, banking, working and playing in different countries (so, for instance, the country that thinks it has the right to tax you isn't the one in which you earn your money).

Sound like something just for the super-rich? It always has to me, too. But as many as one million expatriate Americans now live some variation of the PT life, and many have created simplified versions of it for themselves.

Read all about it:

Here's an interview with Harry Schultz who, along with Dr. W.G. Hill, is usually credited with inventing the PT concept:

www.cyberhaven.com/libertarian/pthist.html

For many years, Scope International offered the most well-reputed (and very expensive) publications from a freedom perspective on living and doing business abroad. Titles include *PT: The Personal Traveler, PT2: The Practice,* and related books like *Banking in Silence, the Channel Island Report, the Malta Report, Tips and Traps of Going Global,*

Portable Trades and Opportunities, and *The Passport Report*.

These reports are still available at reduced prices from Eden Press (www.edenpress.com). The offshore freedom picture changes rapidly as the U.S. government extends its global arms and eyes, but many of these books still contain valuable information.

EscapeArtist.com, mentioned in Item 49 as an offshore business resource, is also a superb offshore living and traveling resource. Particularly look at the many, many country profiles and Gallo's own book *Escape From America*.

You'll find links to offshore living, offshore jobs and offshore investments, hundreds of country profiles and Gallo's own book, *Escape from America*.

As always, verify to your own satisfaction the accuracy of the information and the reliability of the people offering it.

> *In addition, [Patrick] Poole said, a bill called "The Driver Record Identification and Verification Act," named HR 3555 and co-sponsored by Rep. James Moran [D-VA] and Rep. Constance Morella [R-MD] has already been introduced in the House. While it is languishing in committee at present, the bill seeks to mandate the creation of a national motor vehicle operator database by combining all state driver license registration databases.* — From a mid-1998 news story, just at the time Congress was pretending to be horrified at "accidentally" having passed a bill to convert state drivers licenses into a national ID card.

51. Will somebody please start a free-market ID service?

We must not allow the federal government to impose a national ID on us. In retrospect, our fathers and grandmothers made a grave error allowing their states to impose *any* form of government ID, however innocuous it may have seemed at the time.

But some forms of ID are certainly necessary. When you, a stranger, walk into the bank with a check drawn on a customer's account, the bank certainly has a need to verify who you are. Even in the freest of free societies, there are many times when a business or individual might have need to verify that you are who you say you are, or that you have the training or skills you claim to have. What we need is free market ID, issued by private organizations and not linked to invasive central databases.

Well, we already *have* that, don't we? When I go into Costco, don't I wave my photo-card at the friendly attendant? When you access your e-gold account, they know exactly who you are without having any requirement for your government ID because they have a unique identifier for you — not a universal identifier, such as the government seeks, but one that's unique within their system. At work, the mere presence of your badge makes everybody feel you're a member of the gang.

Unfortunately, Costco and Sam's Club both now want your drivers license and a Social Security card before issuing membership cards — though these "requirements" turn out to be optional if you refuse firmly enough. Clearly, the ID situation is going to get worse before it gets better. Let's hope we don't have to boycott these old friends of free-market ID.

The problem is getting private ID recognized beyond the issuing institutions. This could be accomplished easily if, for instance, some large insurance company issued private drivers certifications and actively campaigned to have their private ID accepted by businesses nationwide. (The company could even offer incentives to get holders to use the card and incentives to get businesses to accept it.) However (big however)... 1) No insurance company is motivated to do this, 2) Being virtual agents of governments any big company would no doubt go in for biometrics, universal Beast Numbers and that whole business in its ID, and 3) you can bet the fedgov would resent the competition — and do what it always does when it believes its turf is threatened.

Our best hope may lie in all the electronic businesses that *do* have some incentive to develop private ID systems — like the electronic banking systems that have need to verify that you are their customer, but *no* need to know the details of your life. (Check out a company called Zero-Knowledge Systems (www.zeroknowledge.com/), whose privacy products include one called Private Credentials.)

In the meantime, we should all shift our dealings, more and more, to vendors that honor their own ID or require no ID. We should deal more in cash and barter than in ID-sucking checks. And every time we run into a situation that "requires" government ID, we should stop (afterwards, if not before) and ask if there's an alternate way of handling the situation that lets us avoid the use of state-issued ID documents.

These people, who do they think they are, saying that their government has stamped out human freedom... We need to conduct a nation wide search for these right-wing... purveyors of hate... — Bill Clinton

52. Perfect disguise #1

One way to get away with many things is to cultivate a mild eccentricity. Not enough to get scooted off to the loony bin, but just enough to make people go, "Huh?"

Now, obviously, this is a sucky strategy if you want to be taken seriously in a public meeting or a letter to the editor. But if you just want to be left alone to do your own thing, the right type and degree of eccentricity — just a slight, lovable goofiness, perhaps — could be an ideal privacy curtain.

Barney Fife, Jim Varney's movie character Ernest, and even Barney the Dinosaur (Heaven forbid) might be good role models. Who could take them seriously enough to imagine them to be up to anything important — like planning the overthrow of tyrants?

I, for one, want to go on record as favoring chaos. Nothing is more precious to me than my freedom. And the Constitution of the United States says no government authority has the right to take it away. I have nothing but contempt for politicians who believe they have the right and the power to turn this country into a police state for any reason. — Joseph Farah, *World Net Daily*, column of July 17, 1998

53. Anno Libertatis

Science fiction writer L. Neil Smith wrote about it, fulfilling an idea by Thomas Jefferson. Science fiction writer Victor Milan noted that Tom and Neil's idea belonged in the real world. I agree. So here it is.

The idea is *Anno Libertatis*, the year of liberty. In his North American Confederacy series, Neil created a gloriously free (and unfortunately fictional), society that marks its years beginning with July 2, 1776 (the real date the Declaration of Independence was voted upon). Thus, our year 2000 A.D. would begin as A.L. 223 and change to A.L. 224 in July.

When I asked Neil's permission to use the idea here, he also commented:

> I used the regular month names, but would be happy to supply my own list if you like. Trouble with that is then you'd want to regulate the calendar, adding a 13th month and making them all the same length, etc., and that way lies madness, I think.

Unfortunately, he's right. The French tried something like that after their revolution, with some lovely month names that translated to "Rainy," "Snowy" and suchlike. Didn't take. (And must not have made people in the southern hemisphere or different climate zones too thrilled!) You could play with names (Liberty, Jefferson, Spooner, Paine, Rebellion, Flower, Freedom, Fun, Death-to-Tyrants...), but unless you're a pope, like the last guy who changed the western calendar, it probably won't stick.

So Anno Libertatis may remain mainly a philosophical statement, rather than something you'd put on an interoffice memo. Still, it's a good one. If you're of the Christian persuasion or like the old date system for any other reason, there's nothing to prevent you using both systems side by side.

In freedom — January 1, 1999 A.D. and 223 A.L.

> *What a waste it is to lose one's mind. Or not to have a mind is being very wasteful. How true that is.* — Former U.S. Vice-President Dan Quayle at a fundraising event for the United Negro College Fund, attempting to quote the organization's motto, "A mind is a terrible thing to waste."

54. Learn from Shirley Allen

In the fall of 1997, in what soon became a *cause celebre* for freedom lovers, a tyrannical judge in Illinois ordered a harmless woman arrested without warrant and incarcerated without trial, at her own expense, just like a prisoner in 17th Century England.

Oh, excuse me, I put that wrong. What I really mean to say is that some kindly relatives, selflessly concerned about a dangerous, yet helpless, madwoman's welfare, persuaded a wise and compassionate judge to have Shirley Allen lovingly taken care of in a state mental hospital. For her own good, of course. And I'm sure it had nothing to do with her valuable property or the fact that she'd made it clear some of those relatives weren't going to get any of it.

Allen had harmed no one, threatened no one and was (at worst) possibly subject to delusional thinking. Her real crime was having a few valuable assets and not being sociable to relatives who may have coveted those assets.

Be that as it may, this "crazy," "helpless" middle-aged widow held the Illinois state police at bay for 39 days before being temporarily disabled by a rubber bullet and tackled by a waiting cop. She was no survivalist, but she survived better than some survivalists might. After cops cut off water, electricity and outside communications to her home — and shot out all her windows, to boot — she was forced to survive in most unpleasant conditions. She prevailed over a tear gas attack and eight canisters of pepper spray, as well. We could learn a lot from this resourceful woman.

Among other things:

- When attacked with tear gas, she had no survivalist's gas mask handy. But she immediately wrapped wet towels around her head and protected her skin with Vaseline.

- She had a large variety of home-canned foods and (this is important) she had them *accessible*. They weren't in a storage shed, root cellar, garage or basement accessed via an outside door.

- She had foods that didn't require preparation.

- She had a bucket to replace the toilet the police rendered inoperable when they shut off her household water. And again, it was accessible.

- The police couldn't figure how she managed to sustain herself so long after they cut off her water. The fools never figured out something that's obvious to a lot of folks who live in agricultural areas or near oil wells (as Allen did). Her water well was contaminated, so she never relied on it for drinking water. She had lots of stored water — and again, all of it accessible.

- She had a windowless inner area of the house into which she could retreat. She made her bed in a hallway during the entire siege, and also retreated to a bathroom during the pepper spray overkill attack. With their hidden sound recording equipment, Allen's would-be controllers eavesdropped on her gagging and retching in the wake of their gas and pepper attacks, but they didn't drive her out.

- She had a radio that didn't require electricity, so she was able to monitor reports on her own situation.

- She was armed. Not particularly well armed, and she had very little ammo. But she had one of the most versatile weapons of all, a shotgun, with which to protect herself and her home.

- Above all, she *thought* like a survivor. I hope Allen someday lets the world know in detail what mental and emotional skills helped her keep going. But certainly she was resourceful, creative and determined. And she wasn't gullible enough to buy into all the nicey-nice messages with which her tormentors tried to induce her to surrender.

An important message of Allen's experience is that preparedness doesn't necessarily have to be a daunting, expensive task. A few simple preparations, when used with the right mindset, are more valuable than $10,000 worth of supplies you aren't able to use.

Oh, if you're ever under siege, you might want to have some ear protection handy. The state police played Barry Manilow to Allen until presumably the noise drove the cops themselves crazy and they quit. Whether that was better or worse than the dying rabbit screams and Nancy Sinatra songs with which the FBI tormented the Branch Davidian children, it's hard to say. But unpleasant noises are a favored method for torture and brainwashing.

Maybe get some eye protection, too, as bright lights are another torture method. But ear or eye protection can be a mixed blessing; either might cause you to miss the signs of an attempted sortie by your besiegers.

Health care with the efficiency of the post office and the compassion of IRS — Internet signature line

55. Preventing a psychiatric siege?

I can't guarantee this will work if the little men in the white coats and jackboots are seriously after you, but there's an organization dedicated to helping people prevent psychiatric abuses to themselves, their children and other family members.

The Citizens Commission on Human Rights will send you, gratis, a document you can sign called a "Letter of Protection from Psychiatric Incarceration and/or Treatment." You can contact them at:

Citizens Commission on Human Rights
6616 Sunset Blvd.
Los Angeles, CA 90028
voice: 1-800-869-2247
e-mail: humanrights@cchr.org
www.cchr.org

By signing this letter you express your objection to commitment and involuntary "treatment" with drugs, shock therapy or whatever the latest psychiatric voodoo rattle is. It *might* help you avoid commitment. But even if it doesn't, it could be useful. If you're committed against your clearly written wishes, there's a *good* chance this document will help you avoid the so-called treatments — though you should also be aware that the control-shrinks have a habit of adjudging you to be ill and dangerous *because* you refuse their "help." CCHR was founded by the Church of Scientology and Dr. Thomas Szasz, Professor of Psychiatry Emeritus at State University of New York and author of books challenging establishment notions of mental illness.

Oh, yeah. After keeping Allen in the hospital for more than a month, during which time she refused all treatment, the doctors said she was no danger to herself or anybody else. Then they sent her a bill for nearly $1,000 per day for their "services." Pretty expensive hotel, eh?

Six months after the siege — which cost Illinois taxpayers, $649,000 — Terrence Gainer, head of the state police, still insisted Allen was dangerous and that he had done all the right things to "rescue" her. The state of Illinois eventually agreed to drop the bill for the hospitalization and "rescue operation" if Allen agreed not to sue. The state should thank its lucky stars it got off so lightly.

> *"Do you pray for the senators, Dr. Hale?" "No, I look at the senators and pray for the country."* — Edward Hale (1822-1909), US author and clergyman

56. Lie to your doctor

Long ago, the federal government took away the privacy of your relationship with your banker. Insurance companies and the government regulations that rule them have been eroding the privacy of your relationship with your doctor for years. But the "health care" legislation mentioned elsewhere in this book (Public Law 104-191) and in other legislation still being contemplated, delivers the *coup de grace* to medical privacy.

Basically, we're getting socialized medicine via the back door. The rejected HillaryCare of 1993 is being delivered by Republicans. Yes, your doctor and your insurance company will still be "private." But they and their operations — and your visits to them — will be so tightly controlled and monitored by the federal government that "private" and "public" will have little meaning.

Among other things, your medical records will be as public as a stripper's backside. So far, there really isn't one central medical database in some marble tomb of bureaucracy somewhere. But that hardly matters when the law now requires *all* medical data to be transmitted and stored using a single federal standard, and requires that *all* medical data about you be kept under your one, national, "unique identifier" (which may be your SS number or some modern replacement of it). Whether there are 50 separate databases or one, your most personal information will be equally available to bureaucrats, crooked politicians, researchers, cops, CIA spooks or whichever connected folks have the pull to get it or the savvy to crack it.

Since 1998, Congress has repeatedly de-funded the medical database and its "unique identifier." However, the Bush administration accepted the mis-named "medical privacy regulations" written by the Clinton administration under the authorization of PL 104-191. The obscene plan to end medical privacy creeps ahead.

Please don't be naïve enough to imagine the central planners will *ever* back off this plan. If they can't get it by going in the front door, they'll get it some other way (as they're doing with the childrens' vaccination database (Item 7)). And believe me, there are *no* privacy safeguards possible.

So what's a private and free individual to do? Lie to your doctor.

Of course, to get the most appropriate care, you need to tell your doctor the full, unvarnished, and sometimes embarrassing truth. So lying to your doctor can get pretty tricky. If you decide lying is the right thing to do, you have to tell her enough to be useful, while fudging and obfuscating other details.

In theory, if you drink a quart of gin a day or habitually have unprotected sex with various farm animals, your doctor needs to know that. If you got injured while doing something risky like extreme skiing, it isn't really nice to say you tripped over your cocker spaniel while bringing chicken soup to your sick mother. If the pain is in the left side of your belly, it just doesn't make sense to say it's in your right big toe, of course. Besides, some of us just aren't good liars. (I'm a rotten one, myself.) And the doctor's going to *know*.

Nevertheless, if your doctor and your insurance company are going to rat you out, you owe them no allegiance. Quite the opposite. It's getting to be that we all have a downright duty to screw up all processes by which information flows into the maw of the fedgov. I'd say you owe it to the cause of privacy and freedom to obscure the data about yourself as much as possible, your conscience permitting, of course.

So here are some kinds of lies — and a few related tactics — to consider:

- First and foremost, wherever possible try not to give your real Social Security number or other identifier. Make it hard for everyone who tries to get it. Lie about it — and lie about it differently — at every opportunity. (You'll have to balance your need to lie against the possibility of screwing up your records so the claim doesn't get paid.)

- This gets harder to do when your insurance company or the government gives you a "swipable" card. So... well, this isn't a lie, but it is a monkey wrench... get out the old magnet and "accidentally" wipe the card's strip or chip.

- Okay, if you're stuck with the number, one way or another, then lie about your address, your age, your middle name, your place of birth — anything to confuse the record. Yeah, the records will still be under your "identifier," but who can be sure they're really yours?

- Go to different doctors. In different cities, if possible. Give each different information about your address, age, middle name, etc. (Again, it gets more difficult if you have to present a card. But never fear — high-tech fake ID mills will eventually come to your rescue.)

- Don't offer any personal information that isn't directly pertinent to your condition. This is very tricky, and it's damnable that any "system" would put you in a position where you had to do it to preserve privacy. But there it is. It's tricky partly because you don't always know what's relevant to your condition. (Did your father's recent death have anything to do with those chronic stomach troubles?) It's tricky because, ideally, your doctor should be able to help you with the most personal sorts of problems. ("Doc, does it sound as if my wife might be using amphetamines?") But the new "federal standards" don't allow you any privacy. Whatever you say is supposed to go into the record, in a form they can access.

- Lie, but lie plausibly, about how you got a certain injury or condition.

- If you know what's wrong and what medicine you need, you might lie about the symptoms, particularly if your real condition is sensitive. For instance, if you're hyped up enough to jump out of your skin and know you want some Valium to get you through a stressful time, you could claim back spasms. Doctors prescribe Valium for both. Don't do this, of course, if you're in any doubt about what really ails you.

- As long as it's still possible, pay cash for small medical problems. Go to a doctor you don't use for your insurance cases and fill the patient information form with false statements. Or just don't answer key privacy-violating questions.

- Find a doctor who'll lie for you. Or who'll agree to keep the most personal stuff off the record.

Of course, when it comes to serious medical conditions, emergencies or long-term care, you're stuck. You need your doctor and your insurance company, and you may just have to put up with whatever goes into the database. And when technology allows something like instant scanning and comparison of DNA records, all dodges get harder. Not impossible. But a lot more difficult.

So try to stay as healthy as you can, use alternative medical providers where appropriate, hope enough doctors get fed up enough to opt out of this snoop system and take their practices underground, pay cash for the small stuff and keep your fingers crossed.

> *To go against conscience is neither good nor safe; God helping me, I can do no other: Here I stand.* — Martin Luther

57. Another possible option for medical privacy

There's another saner, more dignified method to try to preserve your privacy. There's no guarantee it'll work, but if lying and sneaking go against your grain, or if you want to add an extra layer of protection on top of the lies, you might try filing a statement like this with your doctor and your insurance company.

> I, _____, expressly forbid transmission of
> my medical records to any third party, or placement of any
> of my medical data (including records of conditions, medica-
> tions or statements made by me or my physician) into elec-
> tronic databases, without my written consent. I expressly
> forbid the release of medical data about myself to any indi-
> viduals or institutions, public or private, without my prior
> written consent.

You might decide to add some other language to give this
some teeth. And you'd be far better off if you actually got
your doctor and an officer of your insurance company to sign
a statement like this, rather than just making it unilateral.
Good luck on that, though.

Under PL 104-191, unfortunately, you have no right to
make such a requirement at all. The law gives you no choice
— not even the right to inspect your own records to make
sure they're accurate. (Just think what happens to your job
and reputation when someone, either on purpose or by mistake, inserts info in your file indicating you're on anti-
psychotic medication or have a degenerative disease.)

Your medical history isn't your own any more. It now belongs to the federal government — just as you do.

*Remember, as you go along your busy way, to pause
occasionally to take some time and smash the state.* —
Graffiti, ca. 1970

58. Rules for Radicals

In 1971, Saul Alinsky, a famous union-and-community or-
ganizer from the 1930s and 40s, published a book called
Rules for Radicals. His intention was to impart some old-
time, patient wisdom to a young generation he perceived as

nihilistic, co-opted or merely ineffective in its blind rage against "The Establishment."

Bad timing, Saul. The kids you were talking to mostly dropped back in about the time you published your book. Now, parts of *Rules* read like a glimpse into some almost picturesque past.

Other parts are a different story. Despite being opposite to most freedom-movement folks in fundamental ways, Alinsky knew what he was doing when he talked tactics. Try these on for size:

- The first rule of power tactics: *Power is not only what you have, but what the enemy thinks you have.*

- *Never go outside the experience of your people.*

- *Whenever possible, go outside of the experience of the enemy.*

- *Make the enemy live up to their own book of rules.*

He tells how to do all this, too. While not every word can apply to the freedom movement's highly individualistic disorganization, much of this book could be adapted to our use. Perhaps even more important, Alinsky wrote his book at a time when many activists were simply unraveling with frustration at their inability to achieve (or even make perceived progress toward) their goals. We are at an equivalent moment and can use what Alinsky called "a pragmatic primer for realistic radicals" to help keep us on track.

The book is still in print (Vintage Books) and can be purchased from Amazon.com or ordered through most bookstores.

We must combat an unholy axis of new threats from terrorists, international criminals and drug traffickers. These 21st century predators feed on technology and the free flow of information and ideas and people...— Bill Clinton, 1998 State of the Union Address

59. Take care of your computer (and it will take care of you)

As long as the telecommunications system remains in operation, your computer is going to remain one of the most vital freedom weapons in your arsenal. Unless you're one of those people who simply *loves* computers, chances are you take that machine and its functions for granted until something goes wrong. But just as you keep your guns oiled and dry and keep your shooting skills in practice (You do, don't you?), you should take a little extra time to make sure your computer will be ready to take care of you when you need it.

Here are some things to think about:

- Have as many spare parts for the hardware as possible. This doesn't mean going out and buying duplicate components, or an entire duplicate computer. It might mean something as simple as hanging onto your old computers — provided you replace your system every couple of years and not once a decade. With luck and a vigilant eye, you might be able to pick up a "parter" from a used computer store or garage sale.

- Keep up your computer skills. Even a non-technoid should be able to successfully disassemble and reassemble a computer, deal with problems like loose wires and broken connectors, and perform simple diagnostics. If, like me, you're semi-inept, be sure to make friends with someone who's knowledgeable about both hardware and software.

- Keep software together and in a safe place, preferably off-site but still retrievable in a hurry. Since an increasing amount of software is simply downloaded over the Internet and doesn't exist in the form of packages with manuals, don't forget this "invisible" software when making your plans. (That "invisible" software gets taken care of in the next item.)

- Make frequent backups of your hard drives and keep them off site. The location should be (ideally) relatively safe from most natural hazards, someplace the Law wouldn't look, but someplace you can access in a hurry if your system goes down. There are now some services that will let you perform backups over the 'net. But so far these are slow, costly and have other drawbacks that make them less than perfect. Some folks connected with the Liberty Round Table (www.lrt.org) are now offering encrypted data backup services for fellow members of the freedom movement. While I think this is a noble effort, I'd personally be leery of storing strangers' data, and would not place my own data with other political activists, encrypted or not.

- Have several alternative e-mail addresses, both for privacy and in case your provider goes belly up. There are an increasing number of free e-mail services, some of which (like bigfoot.com and mail.com) offer forwarding to another address and some of which (like hotmail.com) operate only on the net. With the former kind, you gain a little privacy (though your real address still appears in the message header and you won't get your mail if your ISP goes down). The latter is clunkier to use, but has the advantage that, if your ISP is cut off or cuts you off, you can log on via someone else's system to get and send mail.

Why are so many people concerned so much about which party these dipshits come from? It seems to me to be an entirely moot point. I usually start losing respect for someone the minute they start talking Democrat/Republican, it's like asking someone whether they prefer herpes or syphilis... — Steve Archer

60. The definition of insanity

Someone once defined insanity as: "Doing the same thing over and over again and expecting it to yield different results." Ask yourself if you are doing anything that might fit this definition. (Most of us are, alas.) Arguing with the same old people on Internet newsgroups? Petitioning officials for your rights? Letting someone manipulate your behavior? Freaking out *every* time some shortwave radio host announces his latest unverified and unverifiable fantasy? Voting for Republicans or Democrats? Buying expensive goodies and expecting them to make you happy? If you are doing something and it demonstrably isn't working, then stop! Don't do it any more! Be still for as long as you have to — until you can think of something *effective* to try.

If my ancestors would have been armed, they wouldn't have been slaves. — J.J. Johnson, militia leader

If my ancestors would have been armed, the Nazis would have been in the gas chambers. — Nancy Lord Johnson, attorney and former Libertarian Party candidate for vice president of the U.S.

61. Okay, so Michael Harries talks guns, too.

Earlier, I said I'd been surprised when only two readers of *101 Things* offered extensive critiques of that book's segment on firearms. Well, as I was finishing up this book, Michael Harries sent a 22-page letter (Are you serious, Michael, a *22-page letter???*), largely dedicated to telling me what a charming and brilliant person I am in all other matters, but how totally wrong-headed I am about everything — well, almost everything — gunnish. I sez to myself, "How the heck am I going to answer a 22-page letter? Even an intelligent, witty, and all-too-insightful one like that?" Then it dawned on me that my best answer was just to shut up and let Michael have center stage. Unlike Parker and Hobbit (Item 46), Michael is a gen-u-ine, certifiable expert on firearms, self-defense and survival. He was an instructor on Jeff Cooper's staff at API/Gunsite for 12 years, invented the Harries Flashlight Technique, and taught "Seminars on Survival" with folks such as firearms guru Mel Tappan back in the 1970s. So I deleted the item I'd already written on Ten Tastee Recipes for Barbecued Gestapo Agent (Sorry; maybe next book.) and made room for Michael to add his expertise to the subject of weapons for survival and freedom fighting.

First, he introduces himself:

> I might be about the most knowledgeable firearms consultant and instructor you will ever run across, because I have spent most of my adult life involved with "survival" type shooting and solutions for people who were not interested in firearms for a hobby... People [from the Seminars for Survival] would contact me for shooting lessons and ask, "Mr.

Harries, if I don't have eight rifles, three shotguns, seven pistols and an air rifle, am I going to die?"

At this point I have to interrupt with some background. Many of the firearms recommendations in *101 Things* were inspired by the recommendations of the late Mel Tappan, from his famous book *Survival Guns*. I failed to give Tappan proper credit then. Now, I happily make up for that lack — but I also let the ghost of Mel Tappan take some of Mr. Harries' heat. Among other things, Tappan did a great deal to popularize the idea of owning a variety of specialized firearms. Harries says this is fine, as far as it goes, but that, "people sometimes try to have too many guns, thinking numbers will solve the problem." He comments:

> Dear old Mel Tappan (rest his soul) has done more than anyone I know to separate all firearms into hunting, working and defensive categories, but you cannot carry everything you own with you into the field every time you sortie, so there must be some overlap of tasks... Try to remember that everything beside your first-line rifle and pistol are specialty weapons, which *might* be useful but not critically essential.

He says I also helped perpetuate one potentially dangerous "Tappanism":

> No, no, no, the shotgun DOES NOT SPREAD SO YOU DON'T HAVE TO AIM!!! Inside of your house, you have to aim it like a rifle! If you place two targets 10 to 15 paces away and 24" apart (try this with a bench rest, so you don't "wander" over to one of the targets) and aim right between them, with any type of bird or buck shot, you probably won't even touch them, or at most have a few little tiny pellets at the edges. And closer is even worse.

In *101 Things* I also recommended that inexperienced shooters read, talk with a lot of people and practice with potential weapons before making choices. Sez Michael:

> Most "new" shooters do not have the skill level and/or experience to make sound judgments on what will be good or effective for them in the long run. You cannot learn the REAL strengths and weaknesses of weapons just by touching them or reading magazine articles. And too much input from too many sources really confuses the issues. Without a road map, people travel down a path that is either much harder or less effective than it could be.

Michael was very good at providing such road maps, as I found out later when I took a three-day class from him. Unfortunately, shortly after this book was written, Michael Harries died suddenly, after a day spent where he loved to be — at the shooting range. So we must all look to others to provide those roadmaps.

I showed Michael the section containing Hobbit and Parker's comments. Because they went into great detail about specific firearms choices, I won't quote his gun-specific comments at length. However, here's one contrary opinion I thought was particularly interesting and pertinent — his comment on arming against soldiers:

> The "party line" on using M16's and AK's because the "Blue Helmets" will be using them is a very simple case of a *sensible-sounding theory that will not stand up to reason!* Here are a few quick arguments against that idea:
>
> 1) They are conscript troops without first-class training... We should be thankful that they are only armed with "mouse guns" [like the M16/AR15 and AK-series weapons]. Because those cartridges all have limited range and power,

which certainly reduces *their* capabilities against all the Freedom Fighters of America.

2) 30-caliber-class rifles (.308, .30-06) have a powerful and significant ballistic advantage over all "mouse gun" rounds, while still being plentiful, and this is very important when you are outnumbered, and have to hit from very far away, or have to hit something very hard!

3) ...The "Good Guys" ...should have all the time from now until the balloon goes up to *practice with a rifle of their own choosing and become formidable with it!* Why should free men accept the limitations of government conscripts? Do we think that government has all the correct answers? Huh? Duh?

4) Captured weapons and equipment could always be used to arm and equip the new recruits to the band, so that they wouldn't go to waste... but basing your primary choice of weapons on obtaining your logistics supply from the enemy... leaves you vulnerable to salted ammo, defective weapons, hidden follow-you-to-your-lair transmitters, booby-traps, etc.

Oh, yeah, in continuing to take me to task for my earlier writings, he says forget those crossbows for alleged "silent killing":

OH, NO, not the crossbow!... Do you know anyone who has actually shot, or seen shot, a human being with a crossbow? Animals react somewhat differently than humans, and almost all humans (except those humans acting in the movies) tend to scream things at the top of their lungs like, "Oh god, I'm hurt, I'm hit! Owwwww, shit, oh God it hurts, help me, please help me!"... A good .22 long rifle to the head is a much surer method of "silent" removal.

However, he does agree that the bows and arrows, or crossbows, could be efficient silent killers of game animals, who tend not to scream, "Owwwww, shit!" when wounded.

Finally, Michael says practice, practice, practice, and:

> I have found that the intelligent application of strength, as it applies to shooting, with proper techniques, requires (dare I say it again) INTELLIGENCE! I explain this to all of my private students, that the leading prerequisites for being a good Combat Shooter are: STRONG MOTIVATION AND INTELLIGENCE...period! None of this eyes-of-a-hawk or weight-lifter-like strength, or any hard-core military experience. I'm a former Marine, trained in the 1950s, so I'm not all that impressed with the pseudo commandos, and over the last 20 years as a shooting instructor, I've trained Navy Seals, Marine Recon, Army Delta, and spooks of different varieties, plus lots of police and SWAT officers. So I know who plays the game and just how well. Furthermore, I know that you must be smart enough to grasp the advanced concepts and be able to motivate yourself enough to do the practice that is required of you, on a more or less regular basis. There is no real "magic bullet" to shooting (well, maybe a little), but mostly just diligent work, intelligently applied.

Hm. Sounds as if that gives us some interesting hope for beating the bastards.

After his initial 22-page letter, Michael restrained himself and sent only a nine-pager after I showed him the draft of this and a couple other segments of the manuscript. I regret that there isn't more time to go into more detail, because he was clearly a man who knew his stuff and was willing to share what he knew.

61A. And Boston T. Party gets the final word

Shortly before *Don't Shoot* went to press, Loompanics asked my fellow freedom-writer, Boston T. Party, to review the book and write an introduction. Boston also asked to make responses to the questions in #46. How could (or why would) I say no to the author of *Boston's Gun Bible*?

One caveat. Michael Harries disagreed with Glock partisanship (mine and Boston's) and the use of specialty ammo. Both Boston and Michael had excellent empirical reasons for their choices. That's the way it is in the firearms world, were issues are complex and passions about them run high.

You can find Boston (and his books) at:

www.javelinpress.com

Here are his answers, in his own words:

1. The 4:00 a.m. kick at the door

For rural dwellers, a .308 FAL rifle with Sure-Fire flashlight attached. (An AR-15 would be my second choice.) For bee-hiving city folk, a 12-gauge pump shotgun (Remington 870 or Winchester 1300), also with said light. In short, any reliable long gun *with attached light* would serve well. Remember, it's 4:00 a.m., so the lights will be out (or at least dimmed). You must *never* shoot at what you cannot identify, thus a quality light source is vital.

2. Fighting blue berets in the woods

An FAL, which is (all things considered) superior to the M1A and H&K91. Regarding caliber, the .308 will penetrate 12 inches of tree at 100 yards, while the .223 or 7.62x39 will not. Also, I'd have an extra 300 yards of effective range on the Bad Guys in Baby Blue. *Heh*!

A Steyr Scout Rifle (also in .308) would be a fine second choice.

3. Surviving by hunting

Living off bird hunting is inefficient given shotgun ammo's poor weight/meat ratio. Therefore I would *not* choose a combination long gun, much though I like them.

I would pack a Steyr Scout Rifle. The concept is brilliant, the rifle superb, the caliber is up to just about any task in proper hands, and .308 ammo is available everywhere. If you can't reliably take game with this rifle and proper ammunition for the specific task, then the fault is *yours*.

If you *insist* on a combo gun, a Savage .30-30/12-gauge with finish by Robar of Phoenix. Cartridge adapters (to .32 ACP) and shotshell adapters (to 20-gauge and .410) from MCA Sports. Quality sights (e.g. Lyman, Weaver, etc.). A trigger job. Sling. (Note: These are *not* tack-driving accurate guns, and the .30-30 is limited to 75-100 yards on large game, but this is offset by their sheer versatility, and a hunter's good stalking skills.)

4. The only-one-gun scenario

No such thing. A rifle is too long to conceal, and a handgun is not powerful enough to reliably hunt with. Unless you're constantly in the woods, the *concealability* issue is paramount, so a handgun edges out a rifle. I'd choose a semiauto (for its ruggedness and magazine capacity), which means (for me) a Glock. I'd then go 10mm (which approximates the .41 Magnum), meaning the Model 20. (The compact Model 29 just doesn't have the barrel length that a 10mm needs, and gives only .40S&W velocities.) If a 10+"

barrel were available, I'd have one for hunting (along with a shoulder stock).

For a rifle, I'd have an FN-FAL with 16¼" barrel and folding paratrooper stock. This could be concealed under a coat. Muzzle blast, however, would be tremendous.

5. The woman in the car

Her *"crawly feeling"* over an approaching stranger translates to Condition *Orange*! That means, given the concealment of being inside the car, *she should draw and hold her pistol.* (Once, an oncoming car ½ mile away suddenly swerved to the shoulder, and its driver boldly emerged to flag me down. I went to Orange, drew my pistol and held it below the open window as I spoke to him across the road. It turned out that he was late for his flight, and had missed the airport turnoff. A totally benign situation, as is usually the case, but I was ready for foul play.)

That pistol should be 100 percent reliable, powerful, and easy to train with — meaning a Glock in .40. (Not the anemic 9mm. The .45 is only five percent more effective than the .40, but with 20 percent less magazine capacity — not a tradeoff I'd make, even though I like and own many .45s. If you prefer the .45 over the .40, then get a Glock 30.) I'd pick the compact Model 23 over the micro Model 27, as it's easier to train with, and the 23 wears/conceals nearly as well. Full-metal-jacket (FMJ) loads are the most reliable, but without the stopping power of MagSafe, Glaser and other specialty defensive rounds. Go with the Glasers, which feed/function flawlessly with a proven history of excellent stopping power. (MagSafe ammo stops a bit better, but at the *theoretical* risk of less-than-perfect reliability, given their non-rounded bullets, though I've *never* experienced any malfunctions.) Also, have a 6-Z SureFire flashlight and spare loaded magazines.

6. Other comments

Order my book *Boston on Guns & Courage*. Try out many different handguns, but focus on the Glock. Buy *quality* holsters and gear. Go to Thunder Ranch for Defensive Handgun 1, *immediately*. Practice at *least* once or twice a month. Carry your handgun *everywhere* you can get away with doing so. Join Gun Owners of America (www.gunowners.org). Convert your unarmed friends. Then get an AR-15 or FAL and go back to Thunder Ranch for Urban Rifle (and Defensive Handgun 2 and 3).

Thus spake Boston.

Now enough about guns. Next time, I'm writing a cookbook. I don't actually know that much about cooking, but cooks are a lot less opinionated than gun devotees. And a cookbook will give me the opportunity to include those recipes for Stormtrooper with Mesquite Sauce.

Stocks have reached what looks like a permanently high plateau. — Irving Fisher, Professor of Economics, Yale University, 1929

62. The Free State Project

Would you allow other freedom lovers to determine, by vote, what state of the nation you were going to live in?

Probably not. But would you abide by such a vote if the outcome was taking over political control of the chosen state in the cause of freedom?

That's the concept behind the Free State Project (www.freestateproject.com/). The brainchild of Yale political science grad student, Jason P. Sorens, the FSP is some-what more than just another fanciful libertarian freedom scheme.

In July 2001, Sorens conceived the idea that if a critical mass of freedom lovers got together and moved to an under-populated state they could "not only eradicate authoritarian state laws, but slowly wean ourselves off federal control, un-til we reach a satisfactory level of autonomy, whether inde-pendence or something less." He thinks freedom lovers could make a huge impact with as few as 20,000 people in a state with less than 1.5 million people or 600,000 voters.

Others have thought of this before. But their "plans" have rarely amounted to anything more than, "Hey, guys! Let's all move to Wyoming!" (And do what for a living? Harvest sagebrush?)

Sorens and company, on the other hand, are studying state employment profiles, gun laws, marijuana laws, ratio of fed-eral handouts per state, livability, campaign spending, and other vital-to-life factors. And they haven't picked some desolate hellhole, either. They've targeted several potential locations that fit the desired profile, including Delaware, South Dakota, New Hampshire, among others. (The early voting has New Hampshire in the lead.)

Sorens originally gave the project five years and a fifty-fifty chance to reach that critical mass of 20,000. September 11 disrupted the tremendous momentum the project had ac-quired in its first few weeks, but the serious, long-term effort is still going on.

I'm not endorsing this project, though I find it interesting and impressively put together. But without doubt, the free-dom movement needs communities and institutions of its own (beyond the Internet community, which is great, but can only go so far). We need privacy-respecting banks, truly free markets, free choices in health care, and other elements and institutions that support individual freedom, if such a thing is possible.

A free state, vigorously exercising its Tenth Amendment rights while scrupulously respecting the other nine articles of the Bill of Rights, might just give free people enough protection to establish such things and show the rest of the world what can be done when you quit assuming that you've got to *make* people do anything some politician decides is good for them.

63. Alternatives to banking

There are plenty of reasons not to have a bank account; Regimentation, lack of privacy, big fees, dislike of giving a Social Security number, bad credit, and more.

But of course not having a bank account, especially a checking account, is hard. Without one, it's inconvenient to cash a paycheck, pay bills, make large purchases, get a loan, rent a car, grab a quick handful of cash while away from home, or even cash a modest Christmas check from Granny.

Still, the Federal Reserve estimates that nearly 13 percent of all American households (nearly one out of seven families) don''t have checking accounts. And clearly, these people are finding ways to get along.

Here are a few of those alternatives, along with key factors to consider. (And please be aware of the government's ever-changing cash-transaction reporting thresholds — which currently range from $750 (for wiring cash overseas) to $10,000, depending on the type of business you're dealing with and they type of transaction you're making.)

Cash: The advantages and disadvantages of using cash are well known. Here's something else to consider. Radio-frequency ID chips are now so small that they can be woven into the fibers of currency, making all bills individually identifiable and electronically trackable. Euro notes are to be chip-equipped by 2005. Watch for the U.S. to follow suit.

Postal money orders: Money orders are available at every post office in the U.S. At 90 cents apiece, they're a relative bargain. Hand over your cash and walk out with a slip of paper in the amount of your choice (up to $700 per money order), which you can send to creditors or use to make purchases. Beneath the reporting threshold (currently $3,000), the buyer of a postal M.O. can remain anonymous. Only the person who cashes an MO must identify himself.

This is generally a safe way to send money through the mail, as long as the "to" line is filled out; otherwise an MO is a bearer instrument and can be cashed by anyone who gets his hands on it. If you cash money orders at your local post office where your face is familiar, the clerk probably won't require ID. Asking to be paid with a money order with the "to" line left blank enables you to pass the MO along to someone else with no record that it was ever in your hands. Remember, bank MOs and store MOs have different sets of rules than the always versatile postal MO.

Beware: The U.S. Postal Service is soon to implement a system that will enable it to track, in real time, the course of any money order as it is cashed or deposited. This computerized system will automatically notify law enforcement of any transaction that looks "suspicious."

Neighborhood check-cashing services: They're every-where — those storefront operations that cash your paycheck or give you a mini-loan. They enable you to cash checks without having to have a bank account. But they'll charge anywhere from 1 to 6 percent of the face value of the checks they cash. And they do keep records on you, including (in almost all cases) your Social Security number.

Be careful. They're increasingly regulated and scrutinized because the federal government views them as tools of Evil Drug Lords and Foreign Terrorists, who supposedly send hundreds of "runners" to launder billions of dollars in tiny chunks.

Direct-deposit debit cards: Something relatively new: ATM cards without checking accounts. There are several different types. Some enable any company from which you regularly receive money to deposit your paycheck direct to a card-only account. Others can be purchased pre-loaded with funds (like phone cards). You can then use your card to get cash from an ATM, to buy things, or pay bills.

They're simpler and cheaper than opening a checking account. Easy and safe to carry. Ideal for people who've been refused bank accounts, since there's no refusal based on past records.

As with other ATM cards, these create a record of every transaction. If privacy is a concern, use them only to get untraceable cash from the ATM, not to make purchases. Many card sellers still want your blankety-blank Social Security number before issuing a card. While all these cards can be used to get cash at ATMs, some have a limited capacity for making purchases, so understand your card vendor's terms well before you sign up.

Offshore debit cards: Okay, this one usually involves having a bank account. The difference is that the bank doesn't make regular reports to the U.S. government because it's in the Bahamas, on the island of Jersey, or perhaps even in Latvia (yes, Latvia, which is aggressively aiming to be the poor man's offshore banking haven).

There are two broad categories of offshore debit cards:

- Conventional debit cards associated with an offshore bank account
- Anonymous cards using only a number, not a name. These you purchase pre-loaded and rechargeable, like U.S.-based cash cards.

The good: Although your transactions are recorded, the record is less accessible to snoops because it's under the jurisdiction of a foreign government. The cash that backs the card is also harder to grab. In some cases, you can transfer funds into an offshore card account very easily and inexpensively via an online service like e-gold (http://www.e-gold.com/).

The bad: Anonymous cards may cost several hundred dollars to purchase, and they may be useable only at ATMs, not at point of purchase. Don't imagine that your money is invisible, simply because it's offshore. The U.S. government has a long arm and a heavy hand — and the IRS recently ordered all major credit card issuers to hand over their records on *all* Americans possessing offshore credit cards.

The ugly: The term "buyer beware" could have been invented for purchasers of offshore financial services. Check out any offshore financial institution with officials in the country, experienced customers, or a reliable financial privacy newsletter whose publishers do hands-on research. Know whether your chosen country has treaties with the U.S.

that require it to disclose financial data for any reason other than investigation of major crimes.

64. Fun with databases

A nice database programmer named Julia once shared a little story, which I pass along with some elaborations of my own.

Muffy and Buffy Swenson are twins whose SSNs are one-digit apart. Sometimes they're also known as Tuffy or Fluffy or Cuffy or Duffy.

Buffy is female, but sometimes marketers get the idea that she's big, rough, tough Buff.

Cuffy lives on Darryl Road and Muffy lives on Darrell Road and Tuffy lives on Daryl Lane. But is Cuffy's address 777 or 111? Or 177 or 171? And does Tuffy live at No. 8 or No. 3? It's hard to tell.

The government doesn't like you lying ...er, making honest mistakes... on its forms. But as genial genius Julia (aka Julie, Juli, Juley, Julee, Juwlee, etc.) points out, "On unofficial forms, you need no excuse at all. They shouldn't be collecting the data to snoop on you and serve them right if they muck up their database with it!" If you're selective about telling the truth only where the law requires it, the database warehousers won't know that the "'Pine Tree Road' on your gun form 4473 is absolutely correct and 'Pine Tree Lane' on your purchase of wood chips from the nursery is wrong."

Be prepared. — Boy Scout motto

65. Be smarter than I was

Oh, I thought I was so smart!

We were expecting a big storm here in the Northwest woods, but I, Ms. Preparedness, wasn't worried. I had everything I needed, including a new butane camp stove recently purchased to replace one that had served long and heroically. The day before the storm, buying extra gas canisters, I joked to the clerk at the hardware store, "I'm all prepared. That means nothing will happen. If I weren't prepared, then we'd get hit with the storm of the century."

Well, that night it began to snow. After snowing several inches, it began to rain. After the rain had turned the snow to mush, the wind began to howl. Somewhere in the darkness far away, trees crashed — and so did the power grid. Though I live in an area of unusually reliable power, the grid remained dark and cold. And because this is a traditionally all-electric area, the loss of the grid meant the loss of heat, warm showers, ovens, ranges — everything.

Predictably, there were dozens of fools queued up at the hardware store that morning. There, under a single generator-powered light, with a single, generator-powered cash register recording purchases, they scrambled for Coleman stoves, batteries, propane canisters, white gas, lamp mantels, lanterns, flashlights and other necessities they should have had all along. One desperate soul even bought an $800 generator. (Can you imagine waiting until your power goes out to make an $800 emergency purchase?) I felt so superior.

No. Nah. Lie. Not true. Big lie. I felt so *foolish*. Because there I stood with the other village idiots, under the third-degree glare of that one naked bulb. There I stood with my *defective* butane camp stove. When I had attempted to screw the injector into the canister to make my morning tea, the stove had simply spewed butane, thanks to a broken rubber gasket. It ended up sitting in the rain, venting gas, as I endured a cheerless, tealess breakfast. I had committed a cardinal sin; I had failed to check my equipment.

Fortunately, I was able to replace the stove before my fellow fools stripped the shelves. Six hours later — as I write all this on a yellow legal pad instead of a computer — I'm warm and cozy in my house, enjoying a crackling fire. Yes, it happened just this morning. Thanks to my other preparations, I'm comfortable, surrounded by light and ready to sit out what my battery-powered radio says could be days of flooding and darkness. But it is by sheer luck — sheer, blind, *dumb* luck! — that I, Ms. Preparedness, will also enjoy warm soup and hot tea for the duration of the emergency.

Two embarrassingly basic lessons:

1. Check your equipment. Then check it some more. Check it when you buy it. Check it again when you know you might need it. Also, check it on a regular schedule, every year or six months, or at the beginning of your area's rough seasons.

2. Revel in redundancy! If you can afford it, buy extras of all critical items. And check them, too! And don't forget to buy fuels, spare parts and other items needed to operate your equipment.

Don't learn your lesson the hard way — as I did. Or to put it another way, "Do as I say, don't do as I did."

Hey, the lights just came back on! How long do you suppose this little blessing will last, as the rain continues to drum and the wind cracks the trees?

A different way of living is to live in freedom by co-operating with others so that the rules of your lives together are set by yourselves. — Karl Hess, *Community Technology*

66. Your name belongs to you

Did you know that your fixed, inheritable surname was probably imposed upon some ancestor by a government — a government whose motive sounds pretty familiar: to better tax, conscript, and control the populace?

Until the middle ages, you might have had a first name and a highly changeable byname describing your appearance, location, trade, or some other attribute. Depending on who was speaking, in other words, you might have been John Bigge, John Bywater, or John Innkeeper. But these names weren't passed along from generation to generation, and you could change them at will. One individual might have shown up in seven different records under seven different names.

What delightful chaos — a chaos that served the individual while thwarting state attempts to track and manage him.

Fixed surnames were first championed about 1000 A.D. by Venetian bankers, wanting to keep better track of who owed them money. The custom gradually spread across Europe. In some places fixed names were adopted more or less voluntarily (in the same sense your social security number is "voluntary;" you won't be arrested for non-cooperation, but life will be hell if you resist). In other places they were imposed by brute force. The Jews of Germany and Russia, for instance, were compelled against their religious traditions to adopt fixed surnames, and those who refused to cooperate, or didn't have the money to pay for attractive names, were stuck with insult names like Schmaltz (grease), Eselhaupt (ass's head), or Kanalgeruch (canal stench).

In the English common law tradition, conversely, your name is considered your property, and you have the absolute right to change it at will unless you are a prisoner or are using the change to commit fraud. Common law, unlike much U.S. statute law and all regulation, is based on the assumption that you're innocent until proven guilty. Therefore a name change is an innocent act unless proven otherwise.

In all but a handful of U.S. states, this common law tradition still prevails. While you *can* change your name in court, you can also just up and change it as you please.

This might be a dandy thing to do to help frustrate the data-grabbers and identity controllers.

Here's how to go about it:

The first step in making a common-law name change is to start using your new name. Tell your friends, relatives, and business associates (and keep reminding them when they forget). If you're one of the rare beings who moves through the world without paperwork that's all you have to do.

If you're like most of us, ensnared in documentation, step two is getting documents and accounts changed over to the new name. You may be surprised to discover that some businesses won't ask you for any documentation of the change. Most will, however.

So one of the earliest things you'll want to do is get a key ID document, like a drivers license, passport, or company ID switched to the new name. (It doesn't have to be a government ID, as long as it can be recognized as legit and official.) To do this, you may need to submit a notarized affidavit of name change (draw it up yourself or use a form the business or agency gives you; it'll cost only a couple of dollars to have it notarized).

I once knew someone who made up a new name while standing in line at the DMV and got that name put on her license without any documentation. She didn't even get a raised eyebrow from the clerk. But that was in the olden days, a couple of years ago. You probably couldn't do that now.

Once you have a key ID document, it's smooth sailing to change all your credit cards, bank accounts, wills, trusts, etc. It just takes time. And remember, as long as you're not committing fraud, there's nothing in most cases that says you must stop going by two different names, or that you can't possess accounts or documentation in both names.

I'm supposed to add here that I'm not a lawyer and none of this is legal advice. Verify everything for yourself before proceeding.

> *Airplanes are interesting toys but of no military value.* — Marechal Ferdinand Foch, Professor of Strategy, Ecole Superieure de Guerre

67. Drive, ride, fly...?
A correspondent, Eric Oppen, brought up an excellent point. What if you faced an emergency, needed to travel — and couldn't master the only transportation available? It doesn't take a nationwide crisis to put you in this dilemma. I saw my own mother face this one day when she was forced to lurch across town in a stick-shift car when she only knew how to drive an automatic. (She made it, but it wasn't pretty.) Or what if, as Eric asked, you had to hop on a motorcycle?

You owe it to yourself to master as many types of transportation as you can, with special emphasis on those you're most likely to be stuck with in an emergency. So look around you. What kinds of transport are used in your area? Which of those are most likely to be there when you need them?

Think hard! Your choices aren't always obvious. In some places (like parts of Pennsylvania, Iowa and Minnesota) an Amish horse and buggy may be a likely option, however odd that might seem to anyone else. Consider:

- ☐ Walking
- ☐ Canoe
- ☐ Sailboat
- ☐ Kayak
- ☐ Rowboat
- ☐ Motorboat
- ☐ Larger motorized boats
- ☐ Motorcycle
- ☐ Motor scooter
- ☐ Off-road vehicle
- ☐ Snowmobile
- ☐ Stick-shift automobile, light truck, SUV or van
- ☐ Automatic shift automobile, light truck, SUV or van
- ☐ Light aircraft
- ☐ Ultralight aircraft
- ☐ Horse (western, English, bareback, etc.)
- ☐ Horse and wagon
- ☐ Mule
- ☐ Donkey

- ☐ Tractor-trailer rig
- ☐ Delivery truck (various designs)
- ☐ Bicycle
- ☐ Large tricycle
- ☐ Golf cart
- ☐ Tractor
- ☐ Other mobile farm equipment
- ☐ Forklift
- ☐ Road construction equipment

Obviously, it isn't realistic for anyone to master all these. Some types of transportation might be so unrealistic for you there's no need even to consider them. But you should master as many forms of transportation as you realistically can. And don't forget the details (like learning how to saddle that horse or rig that sailboat).

Consider having a few low-tech alternatives on hand. Speaking of which, here's an interesting variant on a bicycle another correspondent, David B. King, discovered and told me about. This company sells four-wheel, peddle-powered, street-legal vehicles, in two-seat and four-seat versions. Kind of expensive, but they're versatile and aren't going to require any scarce fossil fuels or arcane skills in an emergency:

Rhoades Car
125 Rhoades Lane, Dept 13553
Hendersonville, TN 37075
voice: (615) 822-2737 ext. 13553
www.rhoadescar.com

If I had thought about it, I wouldn't have done the experiment. The literature was full of examples that said you can't do this. — Spencer Silver on the adhesive for 3-M Post-It Notepads

68. Running your diesel on veggie oil

When I first heard about this, in a funky little phreakers' zine, I thought, "Now *there's* a nice way to destroy your Mercedes!" But apparently, it's true. Europeans have been running diesel engines on "biodiesel" fuels, made partially with vegetable oil, for many years. In this country, the University of Idaho has been testing biodiesel, made from rapeseed oil (canola oil), since 1979. Other schools and scientific institutes have been investigating it, as well. There's even something called the Veggie Van, which tours the U.S. on vegetable fuel and even has its own Web site. Josh and Kaia Tickell, who designed the Veggie Van, have written a book called *From the Fryer to the Fuel Tank: How to Make Cheap, Clean Fuel from Free Vegetable Oil.*

Now you might wonder why this would interest you. Because most veggie oil, of course, isn't "free." It's more expensive than gas-station diesel fuel. But if hard times come and that diesel fuel isn't there any more, it might still be feasible to get oil from locally grown crops. And, since you can turn used cooking oils into biofuels, you might be able to run a diesel generator, truck, boat or other small diesel motor off someone's remnants.

Idaho researchers say it burns pretty clean, results in only "low to no" degradation of engine performance, and doesn't require engine modifications. While most "recipes" require going to some trouble to produce an acceptable fuel, I saw one report on the 'net of a high school girl running a small engine on a simple countertop mix of 80 percent veggie oil and 20 percent diesel fuel. (No info on the long-term effects of this.)

Mind you, I haven't been able to talk anyone I know into putting Wesson Oil — or anything resembling it — into his fuel tank! I'd try it on a small engine before I put it in my tractor. But for what it's worth, here are sources of more information:

From the Fryer to the Fuel Tank, by Joshua Tickell, edited by Kaia Tickell, 1-888-822-6657, BookMasters, Inc., P.O. Box 388, Ashland, OH 44805, $24.95 plus $5.00 shipping.

Veggie Van Web Site (where you'll also find online ordering info for the book)

www.veggievan.org

University of Idaho Tests Biodiesel

www.uidaho.edu/bae/biodiesel

One can achieve certainty only by amputating inquiry. — Marvin Minsky

69. Most important survival tool to own
Brain: equipped with right attitude.

The militia are the citizen soldiery of the country, as distinguished from the standing, or regular army. The militia system has been allowed to fall into partial decay, showing that the people have little fear or need to defend themselves by force of arms against their government. — Andrews Manual of the Constitution, 1887

70. Be a "Cell of One"

Mr. Morris Dees became quite wealthy exploiting the misfortunes of poor minority people through his Southern Poverty Law Center. Mr. Dees' lifelong expertise at fund-raising has made him and his SPLC fabulously rich, while the poor blacks and others he claims to help may get a few thousand dollars from the courtroom "victories" Dees and his attorneys win for them.

More recently, Mr. Dees has become the nation's chief hatemonger. That is, whenever the media wants someone to define the source of all "hate" in the U.S. they turn to Dees. Dees "proves" (to the satisfaction of journalists, anyway) that there's a neo-Nazi hiding under every rock in America, slavering with irrational "hate," waiting to leap out and kill. A "hate group member," in the Dees lexicon is anyone who speaks ill of the government.

For a long time, Mr. Dees identified Nazis with the militias. Never mind that the militia movement is huge, and your average neo-Nazi group can't draw enough members to raise a good poker game. (At which most of the poker players would be fed provocateurs, anyhow.) But that dodge began to pale, as genuine militia members were arrested for various crimes that turned out to be less than terrifying, certainly not Nazi-like, and mostly committed at the prompting of federal agents and snitches!

When even *that* substandard trickle of militia "terror" began to dry up, Mr. Dees announced, from his infinite firsthand knowledge of the American resistance movement, that the great threat to the security of his pocketbook...oh, excuse me...that the great threat of security to Hillary Clinton's Apple Pie...that the great threat to the unconstitutional government of America... is that most insidious form of "militia group" — the Leaderless Cell. Yes, you got it. Militia groups without groups. Paramilitary organizations without organization. Uniformed loonies without uniforms. The ultimate invisible enemy.

It's perfect for Dees and his ilk, of course, because the alleged Leaderless Militia Groups can't be *dis*proven, any more than they can be proven. Their very invisibility is proof of anything Dees wishes to prove. And their very invisibility is a handy weapon of terror. To Dees' ignorant urban audience, these invisible militiamen are like snakes in jungle trees. You never know when one might drop upon you from the foliage and bite your head off. Picture the liberals, out on their weekend nature hikes, in terror at the invisible militiamen, lurking in the pines and oaks. It would be funny. Except that it's true. And a damn good idea.

Hey, even Morris Dees has to be right once in a while. He's wrong about the Nazi part, of course. But as far as a "leaderless cell" being a very effective agent of early stage, covert resistance, he's completely accurate. What, after all, is the ultimate "leaderless cell"? It consists of one pissed off individual, with brains, skills, contacts, determination and a drive to live free, who decides not to take it any more. It's the software engineer who plants the virus in the IRS' computers or invisibly screws up the data. It's the mechanic who "fixes" the FBI agent's car so it won't run. It's the lone trickster who plants the disinformation with the media, the logger or rancher who takes a chainsaw to the government's barricades. Ultimately, if tyranny continues its march, it's the lone sniper and the silent saboteur and the prostitute who knifes the tyrant's minion in his bed then fades back into the streets.

The ultimate leaderless cell — a very American sort of cell — is the Cell of One. It's him and her and you and me, acting alone in the cause of freedom. Doing what we know best. Seizing opportunities that may present themselves unexpectedly. Taking advantage of skill and serendipity to inflict some small harm on those who would steal freedom.

The Cell of One idea is very "right" for a lot of us individualists. Whether or not you belong to larger, more visible, groups, think of yourself as a Cell of One. Everywhere you go, and everything you do, look for opportunities to inflict covert, untrackable harm upon the machinery of tyranny. Think of yourself as a secret agent of freedom, operating under the best cover of all — the cover of your everyday life. Above all, as a friend of mine observes, remember, "Nobody can infiltrate when you're the only member of your group."

> *"So I've got myself a genuine Rezin [Bowie knife]. Spoils of war and all that?"*
>
> *"...It's the custom."*
>
> *I looked at the heavy brass guards projecting from the handle. "Guess I'll have somebody cut these off, though."*
>
> *"For plague's sake, why?"*
>
> *"Considering all I know about knife fighting, it'll make it easier to remove when somebody takes it away and shoves it up my ass."* — L. Neil Smith, *The Probability Broach*

71. Radios, knives, bugs and other cool stuff

One of the handy-dandiest little devices, and one of the cheapest preparedness tools you can get, is an AM/FM radio with four potential sources of power: household current, battery, solar cells and hand crank. You can get these puppies for as little as $25, or as much as $100, but even the cheapest ones work just fine. You can buy them from a variety of sources, but one that also carries a lot of similarly useful electronic equipment is:

C. Crane Company, Inc.
1001 Main Street
Fortuna, CA 95540-2008
Order number: 1-800-522-8863
e-mail: ccraneco@aol.com
www.ccrane.com

Their version of that handy little radio even has a flashlight in it!

Knives

Some folks say the following is the world's best knife/weapon supplier. (Judging by the claims on its web site, the company itself seems to think so, but independent souls also agree.) These are working knives, not fancy collector things; very well made and durable.

Special Projects
Division of Cold Steel
2128-D Knoll Drive
Ventura, CA 93003
voice: (805) 650-8481
order number: 1-800-255-4716
fax: (805) 642-9727
www.coldsteel.com

Also try:

Smoky Mountain Knife Works
order number: 1-800-251-9306
www.eknifeworks.com

Cool (maybe sort of scary) stuff
Need a voice scrambler? A kevlar vest? A cannon fuse?
Electronic bugging equipment? Handcuffs? Lock picking
tools?

Shomer-Tec, Inc.
P.O. Box 28070
Bellingham, WA 98228
voice: (360) 733-6214
fax: (360) 676-5248
www.shomertec.com

> *Baltimore (AP) Baltimore police have had to rethink
> a gun buyback program after they uncovered a scheme
> to cash in on the program and its $100 bounty by trad-
> ing in cheap, newly bought guns and weapons brought
> in from out of town. "An organized effort to undermine
> the attempt of the program" was uncovered by police,
> said Mayor Kurt Schmoke. — AP report, February
> 1997*

72. Buying guns after the Brady "instant check"
If you haven't already heard how the NRA's pet "instant
check system" for handgun purchases got turned into a nationwide (and completely illegal) registration system for
buyers of *all* firearms, you can read all about it at:

Alan Korwin's Bloomfield Press

www.bloomfieldpress.com/

When the Brady five-day waiting period "sunsetted" in November 1998, we ended up *still* having a waiting period, but also stuck with an FBI database of gun buyers, and a requirement that all gun buyers submit their Social Security numbers (even though no law set any such requirement) before being "allowed" by the government to exercise their Second Amendment-protected rights. We'll say no more about this monstrous, and so-far bloodless, coup. But as usual, we'll have to find ways to work our way around it. Sorry, you poor FFL holders, but since November 30, 1998, nobody who cares about gun rights would ever buy a gun from a federally licensed firearms dealer.

Well, not quite true. Here are a few reasons to buy from federally licensed dealers, post-registration:

- You want to have one registered gun so that if the government decided to confiscate firearms you'd have one to turn in. (This is your "Brady gun.")

- You want to serve as a front person, buying as many guns as possible to pass along to unregistered friends, who reimburse you for your purchases. At the moment, this is perfectly legal in most states — *as long as the person for whom you're buying the gun isn't prohibited from firearms ownership due to age, criminal history or some other reason*. If you're buying for someone who's prohibited to own firearms, that's a crime everywhere. In any case, check laws for yourself before committing to do anything like this.

- You want to do the same thing, but *make money off it*. Say, you were willing to put your name on the line, week after week, in exchange for a buyers' fee of $50-$100 cash. Maybe you could even make a small underground living at it for a while. Until your state or the feddies pass a "one-gun-a-month" law, of course.

- You already have a network of gun owners with whom you can swap firearms. Then when you want that Colt Python, your cousin in another state purchases it for you, and when his best friend wants a Tec-9, you purchase it on his dime.

- You're a complete fool who goes out and buys his own guns under his own name and number, reasoning that the government would never take *your* guns, or that, "I've never done anything wrong, so they won't bother me."

Otherwise, if you want firearms, you should buy from private parties, through classified ads, swap meets, from *non*-FFL holders at gun shows or your local network of gun owners. Reloading your own cartridges is also an excellent idea.

Of course, *all* these methods will quickly be made illegal. It's inevitable, in any case, and it will begin to happen as soon as some tragedy "proves" we "need" more gun control, if not before. Even with the allegedly pro-gun Bush administration, and even after watching thousands die because good Americans aren't allowed to go armed on planes, Congress is still trying to "close the gun-show loophole" (that is, eliminate *all* private sales of guns). We haven't won back a single bit of our Second Amendment rights, even with an administration that claims to be pro-gun. And there's no telling what future Congresses and future administrations will do, particularly after any highly publicized incident of violence.

Tell the truth and run. — Yugoslav proverb

73. Secrets of the conspiracy REVEALED (part II)

Everything is fine. Just fine. The economy fnord is healthy and will grow forever. Your Leaders fnord have everything under control. Your Leaders fnord love you and care about your welfare. What's good for America's corporations fnord is good for you. You will be happy and healthy when you let Your Leaders fnord care for you as only they know how. Don't worry about anything. Everything is good. The television fnord is your friend. Buy everything you see advertised there and you will be happy. You are happy. You are happy. You are very, very happy...[8]

---

[8] All fnords courtesy of Robert Shea and Robert Anton Wilson, *The Illuminatus! Trilogy (The Eye in the Pyramid, The Golden Apple,* and *Leviathan).* Available in several editions anywhere very strange science fiction books are sold. Have you seen the fnords yet?

Chapter Three

In this chapter we consider dealing with nasty times and nasty people.

74. Hallelujah, there's a snitch detector!

Well, yipeeio-kiiiay, somebody's come up with a method for detecting snitches! Freelance snitches, and the government agents with whom they perform their disgusting commerce, have been the bane of groups who are trying to work toward freedom with any degree of confidentiality or secrecy. They've not only put a lot of perfectly decent people in prison, but they've caused people to hurl baseless accusations at innocent associates. It's hard to get anything done when you can't even talk to the guy next to you without both of you wondering, "Who's the fed?" But relief is in sight! Or at least, serious remedy for the symptoms of this psychological fungus.

The prescription for relief is brought to you by "Doctor" Paul B. Dennis, who developed the technology, and "Doctor" Mike Kemp, who administers the medicine. It's voice stress analysis (VSA), a type of truth detection that works by measuring vibrations in the voice. The theory is that our voices vibrate in a higher range when we are stressed, and that there are certain patterns of stress, and therefore of vibrations, that indicate lying. Paul Dennis created his free-ware adaptation of VSA in hopes of reforming government by letting average people *know* when politicians' mouths are spewing bullbleep. Mike Kemp decided to use the idea to identify snitches and clear the falsely accused. So far, so good.

It also turns out, though, that a lot of savvy is needed to analyze VSA results correctly. All kinds of false interpretations are possible if you don't know both technology and human nature. Dr. Mike — engineer, militiaman, jailbird, BATF-buster and student of humanity — offers the savvy. For fees starting at $20, he'll analyze 5-10 brief statements made by you or someone else whose voice you record. Good test statements include things like:

- I have never passed, and I am not now passing, information about my associates to any government agency.

- I believe that it is never justified for a person to inform on his friends' victimless statutory violations in order to escape prison.

- Freedom is more important to me than money or personal security, and I would not trade freedom for either.

- I believe that individuals have the right to do as they wish, without government interference, as long as they are not initiating acts of aggression against others.

For more information on how the process works and how to make recordings for analysis see my article about Mike at: www.loompanics.com/Articles/MikeKempSnitch.htm

To get an analysis done, contact:

Mike Kemp
minutemn@internetpro.net

Mike will tell you the best way to get your sound files or tapes to him.

Now, what you *do* with the snitches you discover is up to you. Mike recommends politely asking them to leave. We're such nice darned folks, I don't know why they're so anxious to bust us.

There's also a program you can buy for $149, called The Truster, which claims to automate voice stress analysis. I'm not knocking the software, which I haven't tested. But from what I saw during my research, there is *no* accurate method of voice analysis that doesn't rely on a skilled, experienced human interpreter. I believe Mike is an expert at interpretation. (Reportedly The Truster showed Clinton was telling the truth when he said he didn't stain Monica's little blue dress; Mike, and later the DNA lab, disagreed.)

Don't trust anyone solely on my say so. That would be folly. However, I'll tell the world that I *do* trust Mike Kemp — for both his smarts and his integrity.

The whole problem with the world is that fools and fanatics are always so certain of themselves, but wiser people so full of doubts. — Bertrand Russell

75. Unfortunately there's no idiot detector

Now comes the bad news. Snitches, contemptible as they are, are only the *second* worst threat to people working against tyranny. In my (in this case not particularly humble) opinion, the most dangerous creature to freedom workers isn't the venomous, verminous snitch. It's the Plain Old, All-American, Garden-Variety Idiot. Unfortunately, idiots are probably even more numerous than feds. And, shockingly, idiots are often found among the most otherwise intelligent and decent people.

Here are the three most telling signs of the All-American idiot:

- Will not keep his mouth shut.

- Will not keep his mouth shut.

- Will not keep his mouth shut.

The common POA-AG-V Idiot does things such as:

- Talks or writes casually about illegal activities he's engaged in, without any purpose to the disclosures other than boastfulness.

- Blats everything she hears about, or sees, others doing, with total disregard for privacy, confidentiality, discretion or common sense.

- Does stupid things like predicting the death of particularly loathsome politicians. (Yeah, it's free speech, but what's the point of it?)

- Comes right out and advocates doing illegally bad things to bad people, in general — like shooting public officials.

- Comes out and advocates YOU doing illegally bad things to bad people. Oh, wow, this is a big favorite. "If you were really a patriot, you would do X." This is the moral equivalent of the teenaged twit who tells his girlfriend, "If you really loved me, you'd..." If he really loved her, he wouldn't emotionally blackmail her. If your friend is really your friend, he wouldn't blackmail you into getting yourself a federal charge for the sake of his own second-hand jollies.

- Constantly harps at others or accuses everyone who disagrees with him of being a plant, a fed, an *agent provocateur*, a snitch or a ship disturber. While you can now send an accused person to Mike Kemp, the chronic accuser is actually more of a problem. (And let's not forget that *one* tactic of a government infiltrator is to disrupt and prevent useful activity. So *this particular variety* of nuisance could be either a POA-AG-V Idiot or a plant.)

- Writes to little scribblers like me, announcing, "My friends and I are fantasizing about [performing illegal and dangerous act X]." Cut that out, guys!!! I don't want to hear it and you shouldn't be telling me.

Even the best people do dumb stuff, at times. But ignorance is curable. Foolishness isn't. Foolishness is characterized by *unnecessary* violations, motivated mainly by the doer's desire to satisfy his own ego. If you spot this kind of behavior, I highly recommend that you stay away from that person, as best you can, from that moment on, even if no specific harm has been done — yet. Until a mechanical idiot detector is invented, your mind will have to serve.

Loose lips sink ships.— World War II slogan

76. Choosing your company

Here's an idea from Carl Worden, liaison and intelligence officer of the Southern Oregon Militia. He says no one — no one — who approaches his group seeking membership is allowed to join. Instead, the group keeps an eye open for people who possess the skills and attitudes they need. Then they recruit those people as members.

Somebody who's eager to join your group may actually be somebody the FBI or ATF is eager to *have* join your group. Beware! This can be true even if your organization is totally aboveboard. I watched a typical libertarian "meet, eat and beat feet" supper club disband after members realized they had not one, but two, plants in their midst. Even though the group was perfectly legit, in fact highly respectable, they were *very* lucky their infiltrators were so obvious. Had those phonies talked just one member into committing a victimless statutory violation, the whole group could have been busted for "conspiracy." Or at least had its reputation dragged through the media. Remember — your guilt or innocence don't matter to corrupt government agencies. All that matters to them is scoring points by busting or ruining you.

Truth is stranger than fiction and also harder to make up. — Author unknown

77. If you *must* talk about something illegal...

This ought to be a no-brainer, but apparently it isn't. The general rule in all things to do with freedom should be "need to know." The only people you should tell are those who have a pragmatic requirement for the information. (And you should be darned careful, even then!)

But what if you simply must — for some very good reason — disseminate (or ask about) some gem of underground activity? By all means do so. But please do it something like this: "What if, in a hypothetical underground in Croatia...?" "I was reading a novel the other day in which..." "I'm writing a novel in which..." "I wonder how those soldiers managed to..." "Did you hear the rumor about the man who...?"

"According to famous military strategist X, it's possible to..."

> *...if they wish to survive as a nation they will destroy that government which attempts to adjudicate by the whim and power of venal judges. — Marcus Tullius Cicero*

78. Trade your guns

This idea has been batted around the Internet a time or three; I have no idea where it originated, but it has a certain charm because of its ability to confound enforce-o-crats: trade your guns. Find a friend or acquaintance, or even a non-FFL holding stranger at a gun show, who's got a rifle, pistol or shotgun similar to yours — and swap. In *many* (not all) states, this is perfectly legal and requires no documentation. But just think what happens on confiscation day, when the BATFreaks or the Village Gestapo come knocking on your door. "The S&W with serial number XXXXX? Oh, sorry, Commandant Klink, sir. I got rid of that years ago."

Until recently, the "moderates" in the gun-rights movement argued that confiscation would never happen in the U.S. Even after Australians and Britons lined up like sheep in 1997 to turn in their firearms, some said it couldn't happen here. Then California Attorney General, Dan Lundgren, announced a confiscation of SKS rifles with detachable magazines. That was a fiat decision, later fortunately overturned. However, in 1998, Massachusetts passed a draconian gun law that required — among other monstrosities — confiscation of many types of firearms from anyone failing to get a state license *to own their own existing, legally pos-*

sessed property.[1] Turn 'em in, folks. You can either do it now because you don't have a state permit, or you can do it later, after you've nicely registered with the government so it knows where to come get 'em during the next round of even more draconian gun banning.

Thus can confiscation happen, even here — just turn up that water under the pot a little at a time, so the froggie-to-be-boiled doesn't notice and jump out. And of course, if some glassy-eyed loony with a record as thick as Bill Clinton's little black book cuts loose and slaughters a nursery school full of kids, a nationwide confiscation could be decreed in a moment of congressional knee-jerking, or even by (illegal) Executive Order. Does anyone doubt that the CIA, BATF or some other proud representative of the federal mentality might engineer a "lone-nut" slaughter just for that purpose? Anyway, these are dangerous-to-our-rights times, and it pays not to have firearms known to be in your name.

Other tactics some people have used:

- Advertise a firearm for sale in the classifieds (where legal). After three or four days, call the paper and say it's been sold.

- Report guns as stolen or lost. Though some have already done this, it is a tactic that should be reserved for the most desperate times. The serial numbers of guns reported to the police are entered into federal databases,

---

[1] Massachusetts Senate Bill 2276, passed and signed into law July 1998. Much of the bill is almost incomprehensible, so that in addition to its obviously draconian provisions, its sloppy language leaves open a world of horrible interpretation. One amusing provision makes it illegal under some circumstances for anyone but a cop to shoot at a human-shaped target. We wouldn't want to injure any pieces of paper or mannequins, now, would we? And here I thought I was doing the good, liberal task of *recycling* when I used that free campaign photo of Newt Gingrich for target practice. Sigh. You just can't win.

after which mere possession of these weapons, let alone use of them, becomes incriminating. A desperate measure for desperate people.

These tactics, like all tactics in this book, are mentioned for purely informational purposes, of course. We good people never break the law. Unless, of course, the law is unjust, stupid and interferes with our peaceable lives.

Those now possessing weapons and ammunition are at once to turn them over to the local police authority. Firearms and ammunition found in a Jew's possession will be forfeited to the government without compensation... Whoever willfully or negligently violates the provisions...will be punished with imprisonment and a fine. In especially severe cases of deliberate violations, the punishment is imprisonment in a penitentiary for up to five years. — German Minister of the Interior, "Regulations Against Jews' Possession of Weapons", 11 November 1938

Individuals subject to this [Lautenberg law] disability should immediately lawfully dispose of their firearms and ammunition. We recommend that such persons relinquish their firearms and ammunition to a third party, such as their attorney, to their local police agency, or a Federal firearms dealer. The continued possession of firearms or ammunition by persons under this disability is a violation of law and may subject the possessor to criminal penalties. In addition, such firearms and ammunition are subject to seizure and forfeiture. — "Open Letter From The Director, Bureau Of Alcohol, Tobacco And Firearms" — Pair of quotes provided by John Taylor

79. Hiding things in plain sight

In *101 Things*, I had a section on burying guns, gold and other crucial-but-vulnerable goodies in PVC pipe. The burying routine is fine for some applications, but it has a major problem if you live in a harsh climate: To keep frost from possibly crunching the pipe and ruining delicate things inside it, you need to bury the container below the frost line; but that makes it difficult to get your stuff in winter, when you might have to plow through four feet of concrete-hard ground!

As I've taken long walks throughout the West these last couple of years, I've seen a lot of other possibilities for caching goodies. While these aren't as secure as a deep hole in the ground, they're easier to utilize, and certainly make it easier to grab your stuff if you need a "getaway bag." Whether you live in the middle of desert Arizona or desert Manhattan, I'll bet there's something similar to one of these within five miles of your home:

- Walking in a desert, I observed hundreds of wind-eroded rock formations. Characteristically, these were undercut at the bottom, creating deep niches, some of which could almost be called caves. A stash could be placed at the back of one of these niches, then covered with rocks or gravel.

- In a heavily logged forest, I found the stumps of old-growth redwood trees. These had been harvested about 100 years ago, at a time when giant trees were cut 10-15 feet above the ground. What's left is rotted and hollow. You could suspend a pack from the top of one of these stumps (inside), hide something under exposed roots, then cover it with boughs and needles, or lay something on the floor of these wooden caves, also covered with boughs and needles. When I first saw these trees, just a few miles from a small town and very near roads, I was sure they'd be play places for kids, or beer-drinking hideouts for teens — very bad hiding places for your crucial goods. But over the several years I observed them, I saw no human sign. Plenty of bear signs, though — so be sure the tree you pick isn't some critter's favorite hibernation spot.

- Exploring an abandoned mine complex, I found a world of hiding places — old shafts, culverts, broken walls, loose floorboards, thickets of weeds and more.

- An abandoned mom-and-pop corner store had loose plywood over a back window and abandoned storage crates and closets inside. You could get inside a place like that and have plenty of time to make custom renovations, possibly including false walls and under-floor compartments.

- An empty house with a broken basement window and another with a loose grate over its crawl space offered easy possibilities.

- A closed factory was surrounded by a chain-link, barbed-wire-topped fence. But the fence had been broken, perhaps in a vehicle crash. It was possible to get inside — into a world of disused furnaces, storage tanks, offices, catwalks, tunnels, junk heaps, dead vehicles and abandoned coal piles — any of which might make a suitable hiding place.

With something like a factory, you'll have to be especially careful. You're likely to be sharing your environment with vagrants who'd happily sell your precious stash for the price of some Mad Dog 20-20 or a hit of heroin. But even in areas obviously heavily used by teenagers or wanderers, I was surprised to find (pretty consistently, if I read the broken-bottle and used-condom signs correctly) that the users tended to cluster around limited areas and leave perfectly wonderful nearby places alone.

Just in case, make two or three caches, if you can, and put them in very different places. Then if vandals — animal, human or government — get to one, you'll still have the others.

For the complete how-tos of hiding things, you can read Dennis Fiery's *How to Hide Things in Public Places* and Jack Luger's *Big Book of Secret Hiding Places*, both published by Loompanics Unlimited.

> *Click, click went the pistol as he cocked and aimed it. "Informers will be destroyed without mercy." We all winced and ducked as he pulled the trigger. It was empty. He threw it on the table with a thud. "Without mercy," he repeated.* — Leon Uris, *Trinity*

80. If the gun situation gets *that* bad...

Guns aren't much like drugs. But the way things are going they'll soon have something in common with crack, cannabis and crystal meth: You'll have to get 'em through the underground or "grow your own" — both guns and ammo.

That means someday they'll be expensive, possibly unreliable, dangerous to get, dangerous to use, etc., etc., etc. It won't be like now, when you can buy them in the open, and be sure of a reliable product. When we've reached the point that the illegal gun trade is as dangerous as the illegal drug trade, the government will no doubt declare a War on Guns, spend a few trillion dollars, confiscate everything from everybody, suspend the Constitution...Oh, sorry, I'm getting carried away. They *already* suspended the Constitution, except for the parts the politicians and the media like.

Well, anyway. There'll be one plus if this situation develops. When you have to "roll your own" weapons you can make 'em really big and mean and strong and really whoop-dee-doo-hallelujah. I mean, if you're gonna hang for having a .22 target pistol, why not hang for having a claymore mine or a submachine gun, instead? Back in the days when guns were legal...I mean, *now*, while guns are still legal (S'cuse me, I got mixed up again.), few people messed with such exotic weapons. After all, what's the motivation, when you can walk into the local gun store and get such a variety of legal weapons? A lot of exotic weapons that the media considers so scary and powerful aren't actually that useful, for ordinary purposes. For the vast majority of purposes, it's actually *better* to have an ordinary, factory-made, common-type rifle, pistol or shotgun. So few people mess with the hardcore stuff, except hobbyists who go out and get special licenses to do it. But when the control freaks have clamped down to the extent of creating a black market, filled with inherent danger...a lot of folks are just going to say, "Well, why the hell not...?"

When you've reached your "Why the hell?" point, it might be useful to have some of the following information on hand. Since you'll also need supplies, it's a good idea to get the books and other information now and start laying in the goods and equipment you'll need. This, of course, *For Informational Purposes Only*. As with all things, you, your ownself are solely responsible for anything stupid, careless, violent, destructive, or too-fun-to-be-legal you do with the information.

First, the primitive and simple:

A zip gun, a.k.a. pipe gun, is one of the easiest projectile weapons you can make. Heck, even high school kids did it, back in the 50s...But I forgot again. That was before they dumbed them completely down. Zip guns usually fire single .22 cartridges, using a nail as a firing pin. Instructions and a diagram for making a zip gun can be found on the Web at:

www.akula.com/~tooch/resist/gun1.html

Spud guns, a.k.a. potato guns, range from water-pistol-sized toys that shoot cut-up potato pellets to six-foot monsters that can blast an entire potato the length of a football field. I've never been impressed with any small-to-medium spud gun I've fired — no accuracy and no ooomph. But I wouldn't want to be standing in front of a six-foot-long spud shooter when it went off. Spud guns are very simple: some PVC pipe, some hairspray spritzed into a chamber; and a barbecue lighter that sets off a spark and causes the hairspray to go "whoomp!" thus propelling a potato or similar object out of the plastic tube. Here's the best site on the 'net for spud gun info and plans:

Backyard Ballistics

www.frii.com/~bsimon/backyard.html

Now, before we get to the serious weaponry, some bad news. 1999 was a catastrophic year for freedom of information about weapons and their use. Because of multi-million dollar lawsuits and new federal legislation making it punishable (20 years, yet!) to publish, in any form, information about explosives and destructive devices that someone might use to commit a federal felony, many books and Web sites on these topics have been pulled. (Paladin Press alone yanked more than 70 books and videotapes.) For what's left, check out:

More sophisticated stuff:
There are dozens and dozens of books on building your own weapons, both ordinary and exotic. The world's best source (and most noted publisher of books on weaponry and fighting techniques) is Paladin Press:

Paladin Press
Gunbarrel Tech Center
7077 Winchester Circle
Boulder, CO 80301
voice: (303) 443-7250
fax: (303) 442-8741
e-mail: service@paladin-press.com
www.paladin-press.com

The following are some titles to look for. Since the first printing of this book, the federal government passed a law that could put a publisher or distributor in prison for 20 years if a reader misused a book on "destructive devices." So while most of these titles are still available from Paladin and other reputable houses, the fedgov's de-facto censorship has made others very hard to get. Good luck (to us all).

Home Workshop Prototype Firearms: How to Design, Build, and Sell Your Own Small Arms, by Bill Holmes

Home Workshop Guns For Defense And Resistance Vol. 1: The Submachine Gun, by Bill Holmes

Home Workshop Guns For Defense And Resistance Vol. II: The Handgun, by Bill Holmes

---

Home Workshop Guns For Defense And Resistance Vol. III: The .22 Machine Pistol, by Bill Holmes

Homemade Guns And Homemade Ammo, by Ronald B. Brown

Improvised Modified Firearms: Deadly Homemade Weapons, by J. David Truby and John Minnery

A Do-It-Yourself Submachine Gun: It's Homemade, 9mm, Lightweight, Durable — And It'll Never Be On Any Import Ban Lists!, by Gerard Metral

Ragnar's Big Book Of Homemade Weapons: Building and Keeping Your Arsenal Secure, by Ragnar Benson

Heavy Firepower: Turning Junk into Arsenal Weaponry, by Ryan K. Kephart

Homemade Grenade Launchers: Constructing the Ultimate Hobby Weapon, by Ragnar Benson

Zips, Pipes, And Pens: Arsenal of Improvised Weapons, by J. David Truby

Many of these books are also available through Loompanics Unlimited.

BANNED

Ragnar's Big Book of Homemade Weapons
Heavy Firepower: Turning Junk Into Arsenal Weaponry
Homemade Grenade Launchers

Inventions like gunpowder, the printing press, and the computer have done far more to overpower oppression than every volume of political thought ever written. — Douglas Casey (as quoted in *Premise Check News)*

81. Liberty Soup

Here's a recipe you might need to prepare when the Brady Law and its inevitable follow-ups get bad enough that you can't get the modern version of this item ready-made at your local gun store. I found it in the July 1998 edition of *Premise Check News* ("Chronicling the Intellectual and Cultural Collapse of Western Civilization"). The ingredients and the mix have been known for hundreds of years, but I've never seen the recipe expressed quite this vividly:

Liberty Soup

1. Mix barnyard wastes, outhouse soil & bat guano with potassium-rich wood ash.
2. Run water through mixture to remove potassium nitrate.
3. Boil solution down.
4. Dissolve solids in hot water, skimming dirt from top.
5. Discard less soluble salts from bottom.
6. Remove precipitated potassium nitrate after solution has cooled.
7. Separately crush charcoal & mix with sulfur.
8. Finally, mix sulfur-charcoal dust with potassium nitrate.
9. Ignite brew and serve to tyrants fiery hot.

It must be remembered that there is nothing more difficult to plan, more doubtful of success, nor more dangerous to management than the creation of a new system. For the initiator has the enmity of all who would profit by the preservation of the old institution and merely lukewarm defenders in those who gain by the new ones. — Machiavelli, *The Prince*, 1513

82. If you have to get sucked into the national ID system...

If, for whatever reason, you cannot avoid getting a de-facto national ID card, having your hemorrhoids listed in the national ID health care database, or being tracked through the Deadbeat Government database, then — when you fall, make sure you fall good and hard. If the government succeeds in taking ownership of your life, then let them have all the responsibilities of ownership, too. Be as useless as a pet Pomeranian. Make them feed you, pamper you, house you and take care of you.

Apply for Social Security disability benefits. Sign up for food stamps. Enroll in WIC. Whine for your Section 8 housing vouchers. Apply for any professional subsidy, grant, loan or payoff you can get. Demand more Medicare benefits. Suck up Medicaid. Tell your troubles to social workers at government agencies, making sure you pay the lowest fee on the sliding scale. Get all the student loans you can. Stay on unemployment as long as you can stretch it. Default on all those government loans.

Don't be deterred by all the recent talk of "cutbacks" and "welfare reform" and "leaner, more efficient government." There's still plenty out there for those who know how to suck it up. And since you're going to be spending a lot of idle time, being a pet of the government, you'll have ample opportunity to research every available benefit, bacon-trough and scam.

If they do make you work, have a career beset by accidents and inefficiency.

Of course, the most desirable course is to stay *off* government ID and *out* of government services. Keep your pride and independence if you possibly can. And for cryin' out loud, don't take the above course just because you're an un-principled cretin who actually prefers to be a leech! But if they get you — if they successfully declare their ownership of you — then, damn them, let them pay for you.

> *"A man can hold land if he can just eat and pay taxes. But — you see, a bank or a company can't do that, because those creatures don't breathe air, don't eat side-meat. They breathe profits; they eat the interest on money. If they don't get it, they die the way you die without air, without side-meat."* — John Steinbeck, *The Grapes of Wrath*

83. "I was only doing my job"

But of course, becoming the system's useless pet Pomeranian is truly a desperation measure. The ultimate responsibility of anyone who truly values freedom and still retains the capacity for independent action is to resist tyranny — personally and vehemently.

If the government succeeds in imposing a national ID card to monitor and control your activities, you should not only speak against the card, you should refuse to get one — even though the risk (in both legal trouble and denial of services) may be high.

If surveillance cameras glare at us in every public place — tracking ordinary folks while criminals and terrorists practice easy means to spoof or evade them — it's going to be up to freedom lovers to monkeywrench the snoop systems if legislatures and courts won't rid us of them. That may mean anything from wearing Groucho glasses to painting over the camera lenses to shooting the camera's little eyes out.

And you'll need to make those same kinds of decisions and commitments about anything else that bids to steal your, or your children's, freedom.

I debated for a long time about where to place this item in the book. On one hand, this is such a fundamental, basic truth of freedom that it ought to be back there in the kindergarten classes. There shouldn't be a single self-proclaimed freedom lover on this earth who isn't willing to say a resounding NO to tyranny every day. But in fact, experience tells me that the exact opposite is true. People who claim to be freedom lovers are often perfectly willing to make all kinds of noise, go to protests or give funds to political groups, or stand on the sidelines cheering while someone else takes a personal risk.

But the one thing most people are utterly unwilling to do is put themselves at the slightest risk — or even to the slightest inconvenience — to live by what they claim to believe in. Those people can stop reading now, because you have to do something that's even harder, if you sincerely want freedom.

If you actually want to restore the Bill of Rights, you must refuse to destroy the Bill of Rights in your daily work.

If you're employed by a government agency that regularly exceeds its constitutional authority to the detriment of freedom, quit. If you work for a corporation whose products or government contracts are routinely used to destroy individual freedom, quit or transfer to a division that does something beneficial. Or, if you're in a position to do it, lobby bosses and board members for corporate-cultural change.

Withdrawing your labor from freedom-killing institutions is one of the most effective ways to halt the erosion of freedom. It's also a good way to maintain personal integrity. Don't close your eyes to the impact of your own daily decisions. Don't stay with a freedom-killing job just because you're afraid of making a change. Don't someday shrug and tell your grandchildren that, when their freedom disappeared with your paid assistance, you were "only doing my job."

> *I had reasoned this out in my mind; there was one of two things I had a right to, liberty or death; if I could not have one, I would have the other; for no man should take me alive; I should fight for my liberty as long as my strength lasted.* — Harriet Tubman ("Moses"), on her decision to escape from slavery

84. Underground railroad: hope of the future?

Quite recently, as the futility of conventional activism and the unrelenting savagery of government has become more obvious, many people have started seriously planning for alternative actions. One of these is creating underground railroads for the freedom movement. Underground railroads already exist in America. There are fairly well-known ones that assist parents fleeing with allegedly abused children, gay teenagers escaping from forced institutionalization and "treatment," and refugees from war and dictatorships to whom the government won't grant official refugee status.

There are already informal underground railroads operating within the freedom movement, as well. But these are generally small and are simply networks of friends or chance strangers helping each other in need. In building more complex and diverse networks — in which strangers, as well as friends, could find refuge, we face problems other networks, past and present, might not have had to deal with:

- Unlike the slave railroad of the 1800s, for most of us there is no safe destination. While some might find refuge in Canada, Mexico, the Caribbean or beyond, there is simply no single spot on earth, today, where we can arrive and say, "We are free." For instance, if we are hoping to flee a state that requires universal numbering, leaving the country will only land us in another country that requires the same.

- Unlike the child-hiding and gay teen networks, we are likely to have the heavy force of federal agencies after us. This presents an entirely different danger than if faced by those who have only state police agencies or private detectives on their tails.

- Any political-movement underground railroad is likely to be heavily infiltrated by government snoops and snitches before it ever gets started.

- While some parents offer rewards for the return of their runaway children, few can offer the financial incentives the fedgov, rich with forfeiture loot and tax money, can offer its snitches for their assistance in tracking down people like us. How many of your "friends," let alone strangers operating underground railroad stations, would cheerfully sell you out for $20 - $40,000? That's often the going price for betrayal, these days.

- ID is becoming harder to fake. It will never be impossible. But we face a far greater technical challenge than those who operated in the 19th Century, or those teens who merely have to stay out of sight until they reach 18, when they can go back to using their own ID.

- Most of us have never really been tested, and too many of us have no real concept of "death before dishonor." Unless we are motivated by inviolable spiritual convictions, as most members of successful undergrounds have been, too many of us may sell out or bail out at the least provocation.

When the day of darkest need comes, many problems will solve themselves spontaneously. Safe houses will be opened simply because neighbors, relatives and comrades perceive an immediate need. Other problems aren't so simple. We need to be working *now* on methods for determining trust-worthiness, on communications, on secure organizational structures, on safe routes, and on access to sophisticated ID and databases. Please think about this.

With the help of some wonderful people who once oper-ated a secret station, I wrote a longer article about forming underground railroads, which can be found in *The 1999 Loompanics Main Catalog*. Still, any article can be no more than an outline. Another promising source of information is Jefferson Mack's book, *Underground Railroad*, from Pala-din Press. And for both useful information and some striking parallels, the best book I know of about the historic under-ground railroad is *Let My People Go*, by Henrietta Buckmas-ter (1941, reprinted by the University of South Carolina Press, 1992).

A free society is one where it is safe to be unpopular.
— Adlai Stevenson

85. A joke that's not a bad idea

It arrived via e-mail, forwarded from a daily joke list. It went roughly like this:

A cop is staking out a bar at closing time, hoping to bust a drunk. He spots one guy who looks more drunk than all the rest — staggering around, unable even to find his car, dropping his keys and almost falling over trying to pick them up.

The guy finally gets in his car, but sits there a good ten minutes as all the other customers drive off. Then he fumbles around, turning on lights, wipers, and finally (as if he just remembered how) the engine. He drives forward onto the grass before remembering how to back out properly. But finally, he manages to pull onto the road to drive away.

At this point, the cop pounces. Lights flashing, he pulls the guy over to the side of the road and administers a breathalyzer test. The test reads a flat 0.00.

"Damn equipment must be broke!" curses the policeman.

"I don't think so," grins the stone-cold-sober "drunk." "It's just that I'm tonight's Designated Decoy."

Hm. Perhaps some freedom-fighting groups could use a "Designated Fill-in-the-Blank":

- A designated government ID-card holder to conduct business on the group's behalf;

- A designated normal family to deflect attention from covert activities going on at a house (e.g., a safehouse, underground railroad station, underground press, free-market ID manufacturing operation, etc.);

- A designated harmless goofball to persuade authorities your group isn't to be taken seriously;

- A designated danger man, whose role is somewhat like that of the designated decoy in the joke — to call attention to himself in order to deflect it from others;

- A designated spokesperson (to keep wilder members of the group from blurting what they should not);

The possibilities are almost endless.

If you believe everything you read, better not read.
— Japanese proverb

86. Be a hacktivist

When you enter the Web site of the Cult of the Dead Cow, you are warned: "This site may contain explicit descriptions of or advocate one or more of the following: adultery, murder, morbid violence, bad grammar, deviant sexual conduct in violent contexts, or the consumption of alcohol and illegal drugs.

"Then again, it may not."

What the Cult of the Dead Cow (www.cultdeadcow.com) actually advocates (in its own inimitable style) is hacktivism. Hacktivism is activism for electronic freedom.

Ten years ago, netizens took it for granted that the Internet was beyond political control and censorship. We've sadly found out that that's not the case. Internet freedom is increasingly curtailed by governments the world over. Hacktivists aim to win it back. Some will use means either fair or foul — and many use wicked humor in their efforts.

Learn more about hacktivism at http//hacktivism.openflows.org or type the word into the Google search engine (www.google.com) and see what you find.

I voted for the Democrats because I didn't like the way the Republicans were running the country. Which is turning out to be like shooting yourself in the head to stop your headache. — Jack Mayberry

87. An interesting fact about auto airbags

Airbags! Those wonderful, government-mandated safety devices (so useful for permanently silencing squalling infants and eliminating puny, undersized specimens from the gene pool) have another interesting characteristic, as well.

A chemist friend writes to say:

> We all know how afraid politicians are of terrorists. It was these same frightened politicians who (without the authority of the Constitution) recently passed legislation that makes certain that all new cars manufactured in the U.S. will be equipped with airbags. What the politicians (apparently) don't yet know is that the active ingredient in airbags is sodium azide. Sodium azide, when mixed with any soluble salt of lead, forms lead azide — the shock-sensitive primer explosive used in bombs since W.W.II began.[2] Making airbags available *at all* is practically an invitation to terrorists to make cheap, and very easily constructed, bombs. There is no small irony in the fact that the same politicians who are so afraid of terrorists are passing laws that (in effect) make possession of terrorist raw materials *mandatory*.

Since the *federales* have rushed to make so many "explosive devices" and "terrorist raw materials" illegal, Congress, in its Solomonlike wisdom, may also have made it *mandatory* for new car buyers to own devices Congress has also *prohibited*. Could it really be that every auto buyer is now *required by federal law* to become a felon???

Faith is good, but skepticism is better. — Giuseppi Verdi

88. Most important monkeywrenching device you can acquire

Brain: Equipped with right attitude.

---

[2] He adds: Soluble lead salts can be easily made. A 50/50 mixture of three percent hydrogen peroxide and vinegar rapidly dissolves lead.

*While hacktivists are lining up along one border, po-
lice and law enforcement officials are lining up along
another.* — Niall McKay, "The Golden Age of Hacktivism"

89. When cryptography isn't secure enough

There are always rumors about the security of PGP and
other forms of encryption. The possibility of present compromise — and the virtual certainty of future compromise —
is one of several factors leading to interest in steganography.

In Greek, steganography literally means "covered writing." In technology terms, steganography is the art of placing
messages into photos, video files, sound files and other files
in such a way that presence isn't readily detectable. These
messages can be in plain text or encrypted. Check into it.
Here are two web sites with good general information:

www.isse.gmu.edu/~njohnson/Steganography/

www.cl.cam.ac.uk/users/fapp2/steganography/

And here's one with links to various steganography programs:

www.cl.cam.ac.uk/users/fapp2/steganography/stego_soft.ht
ml

If these pages are dead when you go investigating, just
type the word into any Internet search engine. There's a
growing body of literature on this and a growing stock of
inexpensive software. Although most of the software is Not
Yet Ready for Prime Time — or rather, not yet ready for
non-technoid users — that's changing.

PGP-user alert: A type of program called a keyboard
monitor can enable someone to steal your password by simply tracking every keystroke you make. These programs can

be installed on your computer secretly (Some are designed to trick e-mail recipients into executing and installing them, for instance.) and totally destroy not only the security of your otherwise uncrackable PGP, but every action you ever take on your computer.

Be very careful. Some of these programs are, at present, undetectable by the typical computer user. To give yourself the best chance against them, always have up-to-date virus protection software, and consider getting a process viewing application to see if any program is modifying your system without your okay. (Visit the Developers Network section of www.microsoft.com to learn more about these.) These process viewers are not very user friendly, but they can detect activity of snoop programs typical virus software might miss.

> *The corruption at the California motor vehicle department is so bad that 144 clerks have been fired for issuing false drivers licenses. Hundreds more are still under investigation.* — John Q. Newman, ID expert, in his essay "California Crackdown"

90. Some novelty ID resources

Governments would be funny if they weren't so brutal. For instance, some of their members actually think that adding holograms, mag strips and computer chips to ID makes documents impossible to fake. Or they want *you* to think it. But that's total nonsense, since the same technologies quickly become available to private people, thanks to thieves and technology gurus. There are now fake ID mills at universities all across the land, using sophisticated computer technologies. Free-marketeers are selling "authentic" state ID, complete with mag strips, to illegal immigrants. You can buy realistic-looking fake ID, complete with holograms, from firms marketing their services on the Internet.

The thing that's more difficult to fool is the database to which modern ID is increasingly linked. My research hasn't shown me — so far — anyone who's come up with fake ID that comes pre-equipped with a program that can fake a valid response from a government database. However, it *is* technically possible to do that. And if it were being done successfully, we wouldn't know, would we?

In the meantime, here's the best-reputed source of "souvenir and novelty ID" in North America. They'll make ID from *any* state, province, country, university or organization you want — and will even add a hologram (for a hefty fee). Prices start at $25 U.S. and go rapidly up for stock designs. Custom work may cost several hundred dollars per card. But they do a good job. For $5.00 they'll send you a catalog.

Photoidcards
831 Granville St.
Vancouver, BC
Canada V6Z 1K7
voice: (604) 244-4926
e-mail: info@photoidcards.com
www.photoidcards.com/

There are also a number of sites on the Web containing templates and instructions for making your own "novelty" photo ID. A whole bunch of them, along with some advice on various other underground topics, are listed in the Google Web directory at http://directory.google.com/Top/-Computers/Hacking/Fake_Identification/

Keep in mind that most pushers of fake photo ID are charlatans, novelty sellers or college kids just wanting something

---

to get them past the liquor store counter. The most honest purveyors will admit that their product is for souvenir purposes only, or maybe good enough to get you past a bar bouncer or let you fool a pickup into believing that yes, you really are an Italian aristocrat. Be extremely suspicious of anyone who claims his ID will get you past a police check. But, you can rest assured that somebody *will* come up with free-market ID that good.

> *At many motor vehicle offices in California, shady characters mill about the parking lot, searching for individuals who might need some "help" obtaining a drivers license or state ID card. These individuals, for a fee of a few hundred dollars, will direct you to a certain motor vehicle department employee, who will process your application without you presenting any identification, or completing any written or driving tests. Many state licensed driving schools will provide you with the same "service."* — John Q. Newman, "California Crackdown"

91. Make some friends at the DMV (a fantasy)

They're going to be making all those fancy high-tech drivers licenses, right there at your state DMV. Maybe even right there in your hometown office. You know, the ones with the digitized photos, biometric measurements encoded, Social Security numbers and maybe even little mini-databases of your life encoded on mag strips or in chips.

Wouldn't it be nice to have a friend at the DMV? A really good friend who'd just do anything for you? (Or anything for money?) Wouldn't it be nice to have some of that fancy, high-tech equipment to play with yourself? Maybe you could even make a little pocket change with it.

On the other hand, if you can't have such fancy computers and gadgets, why should they? Oh, Ned Ludd, where are you now?

> *It's hard not to shoot until you see the whites of their eyes when they are all wearing government-issue sunglasses.* — T.J. Kattermann

92. A prediction about the fate of bullies
I predict that, in the next few years, mysterious attacks against individual government agents are going to increase countless-fold. I'm not talking about attacks against buildings, equipment, computers or agency operations as a whole (though these will certainly increase, too). I'm talking about the simple, basic schoolyard fact of holding bullies to account for their bullying. And please note, this is a prediction. In no way is it a recommendation.

However, it is true that the only way to stop a bully is to let him know that every time he hurts somebody else, somebody else will hurt him. Reliably. Relentlessly. Without fail.

They already know this, of course. And they've long feared we'll figure it out. Why else tape out their badge numbers and wear black masks when raiding your home? Why else do IRS agents use false names while raiding your privacy and your finances? Why else do police and bureaucrats — who collect extensive, intimate data on us — scream bloody murder every time they learn some patriot group or underground magazine has gotten hold of *their* precious home addresses and Social Security numbers, while they're so busy looking up ours? Why else are even such once-innocuous folks as federal forest rangers and HUD officials arming and getting paramilitary training? Of course they know.

Every action for freedom is dangerous now, and I'm not saying it isn't dangerous to attack bullies. It always has been, always will be. Governments have tried to make this more dangerous by increasing criminal penalties for attacks on members of the ruling class and their servants. But so what?

Nobody has to go out in broad daylight and shoot an ATF agent, even though the world would be better with no ATF agents in it. If that same ATF agent suffers a run of mysterious accidents, vandalism, scandalous rumors, financial setbacks, insurance denials or other personal pains she might eventually decide to change her lifestyle. Thus she, herself, removes one ATF agent from the world without anyone doing violence.

No one who respects the rights of others, of course, has anything to fear from any freedom lover. The police officer who works only to stop aggression deserves thanks from fellow citizens. The congressperson whose votes are all constitutional gives no one any reason for retribution. Nobody's going to dis a mail carrier — except perhaps other postal workers, who seem to do it all the time. But boy, as I look into the near future, I sure wouldn't want to be a tax-rapist, a drug warrior, a permit-pusher, a property-taker or a gungrabber.

Sometimes by standing up to be counted you make yourself a target to be shot down. — Anonymous

93. Mutual defense leagues

Perhaps you've heard of Peter McWilliams, the charming author of such books as *Ain't Nobody's Business If You Do*. McWilliams, dying of AIDS and cancer, was raided by the DEA for medicinal marijuana. Among other disasters, he lost the manuscript of an almost-completed book — and thus lost months of irrecoverable time. During his days in jail, he was also deprived of the medications he needed to survive.

In the wake of that catastrophe, another writer, Leon Felkins, suggested the idea of mutual defense pacts for freedom-loving noisemakers. There are a lot of people who, while cherishing privacy and confidentiality, have made the very un-private decision to put themselves on the line for freedom. To speak when we would rather to remain silent. To disclose some of our own "dangerous" activities in hopes of inspiring others. Or perhaps simply to speak out on controversial issues — leading literal-minded enforcers to suspect us of everything we speak about, even when we're only talking theory. This makes us very vulnerable — we writers, militia leaders, third-party candidates, whistleblowers and just-plain-dissidents of the world. Since noisemakers may be especially vulnerable to arrest, legal harassment, confiscation and ruination, Leon suggested we make advance preparations to come to each others' aid.

In addition to any *individual* preps (like keeping backup copies of documents in safe places), groups of half-dozen to a dozen of us might draw up agreements to:

- Publicize each others' cases if one member is hauled off to jail or financially destroyed

- Do what we can to make sure that a captured or impoverished pact member gets needed medicines or treatments

- Care for each others' families or pets in an emergency

- Take each other in if we are thrown into the streets; make backup plans to help an endangered person if our own homes aren't available or aren't safe

- Contact lawyers, establish defense funds, or fund legal work out of our own pockets

- Make efforts to see that an imprisoned person's unfinished plans are carried out (where safe) and that unfinished books get completed and published

Some agreements might also require individual members to take certain steps to protect *themselves*. Members can thus encourage each other in their individual preps, and help assure that they'll be less of a burden if disaster does strike.

Agreements should be fairly specific and be tailored realistically to members' abilities. You can't plan for every eventuality, of course, but you can be prepared to swing into action when disaster strikes, then be flexible in adapting to the particular catastrophe.

Whether the plan should be in writing is another question. A written plan assures that everyone understands what the agreement is. Also, some people will simply take a written agreement more seriously. However, if someone's got a really nasty agency after him, it's possible that such a document could be used by enforcers to retaliate against the whole group, instead of just the targeted individual. And certainly, if your pact contains any illegal elements (e.g., an agreement to help a lawbreaking friend get out of the country), you *don't* want that part in writing.

All in all, though, *any* plan is better than the vague statements we sometimes make about our willingness to help endangered freedom workers. With the best intentions in the world, most of us actually don't do much when someone's in trouble. Sometimes we can't.

Just yesterday, I received a plea from a stranger who claims he went into hiding to escape death threats and false criminal charges from corrupt government officials. He says he was once a prosperous businessman who made too much noise about official wrongdoing. Now he's on the streets, without money, writing from a borrowed e-mail account. He might be picked up and hauled to jail at any time. Every bit of the paperwork to prove his case is out of reach.

And there's not a damned thing I can do about it. For all I know, he may be a pathological liar who invented the whole story. He might even be a government plant, set up to trap soft-hearted suckers into aiding and abetting a fugitive. Anyone who helps him without first documenting his tale is a sympathetic fool. Yet, by the time anyone can document his story, it may be too late for him.

Even if he's a genuine tragic hero, you have to ask hard questions: Before he challenged corrupt authorities, why didn't he set up a support network, put documents into the hands of journalists or lawyers, hide emergency assets or otherwise do anything to protect himself? How much of what happened to him is his own fault?

In any case, once they have defeated you, it's done. You can hope to fight your way back up. But you're down. Have a support network of trusted people, and an idea what you can expect from each other, *before* it happens.

An America with two legal standards is an America with no legal standards. — James Traficant, D-Ohio, September 15, 1998

94. Most important self-defense weapon you can carry

Brain, equipped with right attitude.

Every interaction with the police is fraught with anxiety and danger. There is no relative power here; the police officer has it all. — Robyn Blumner, syndicated columnist for *The St. Petersburg Times*

95. On the non-cooperation of prisoners

Gene Sharp, whose books I quoted earlier, also tells the extraordinary story of Corbett Bishop. During two terms as a prisoner of conscience (a religious objector to military service during World War II), Bishop practiced total non-cooperation with authorities.

Whether one agrees with his stance or despises it, considers him a hero or a fool, it's hard not to admire the courage of his convictions. He believed war was wrong, and he would not cooperate in any fashion with war makers. He announced that "his spirit was free, and that if arresting officers wanted his body, they would have to take it without any help from him." He had to be carried into court, and later into prison. He refused to sign any papers, submit to any prison procedures, perform any assigned work, or make any agreements for parole conditions. He refused to eat, dress himself, or even stand up. For 144 days he was force-fed by tube (a horrible process to endure even once). They paroled him. He refused to cooperate with parole conditions. They threw him in prison again, where the whole ordeal recommenced and went on for another 193 days. Finally, under considerable media pressure, authorities released him — unconditionally.

It's hard to match that kind of story, anywhere. But in our own day we have smaller examples of the same courage and principle. We have members and friends of the Lapp family, who spent eight months in a New York jail on a minor offense because they refused to plea bargain, be fingerprinted or otherwise cooperate with a justice system they believed to be unconstitutional and ungodly. (Their story is told in Barbara Lyn and Rachel Lapp's book, *No Law Against Mercy*.) We have Mike Kemp, who, twice jailed, twice refused to cooperate with the jail doctors' plans for treating (and as he saw it, mistreating) his diabetes. Twice he nearly died, rather than let them administer treatments against his preferences. We have others who, rightly or wrongly, have refused to cooperate in their own defenses, refused to work, eat or otherwise admit jailers' authority over them.

A lot of us are going to end up in jail, or in prison, in the coming years. We'd better be thinking about how we'll regard our incarceration and how we might keep our spirits and our integrity intact. All of the above people made up their minds that there were things they would and would not do. They based their decisions on principle, so they had an anchor in case they were tempted to drift for the sake of comfort or convenience. They all did things that, to people who consider themselves pragmatists, probably looked stupid and impractical. But they all, also, ultimately won out.

Authorities may hate and abuse people who take stands on principle. They may make life harder for the Bishops, Lapps and Kemps of the world than for the ordinary slob criminals who just go along to get along. But in the end, it's the principled people who shine. Even the media, the obtuse media, tends to recognize that kind of principled courage, after a while. And the jailers, much as they may hate and try to punish principle, are often ultimately defeated by it.

> *A strict observance of the written laws is doubtless one of the high duties of a good citizen, but it is not the highest. The laws of necessity, of self-preservation, of saving our country when in danger, are of higher obligation. To lose our country by a scrupulous adherence to written law, would be to lose the law itself, with life, liberty, property and all those who are enjoying them with us; thus absurdly sacrificing the end to the means.*
> — Thomas Jefferson, September 20, 1810

96. The ethics of stealing

How could anyone talk about the ethics of stealing! What an oxymoron! What twisted self-justification! It's wrong to steal, end of subject. Except...

- When you need to liberate government equipment for the freedom fight;

- When you need to get that same equipment out of government hands to keep it from being used against free people;

- When you are monkey wrenching the tyranny works;

- When you are paying back an institution, public or private, that's shown its utter contempt for your rights;

- When you are breaking an enemy of freedom.

If this sounds like *carte blanche* to commit theft or fraud against government agencies or government's abusive business partners, it isn't. First of all, remember, *I* can't give you *carte blanche* to do anything; you are the only one with moral authority over your own life, and my opinion is no more than my opinion.

Also, don't use any of this as an excuse merely to enrich yourself while claiming moral superiority. If it ain't for fighting tyranny, it ain't justifiable. If it *is* fighting tyranny, on the other hand...

> *To summarize: it is a well-known fact that those people who most want to rule people are, ipso facto, those least suited to do it. To summarize the summary: anyone who is capable of getting themselves made President should on no account be allowed to do the job. To summarize the summary of the summary: people are a problem.* — Douglas Adams, *The Restaurant at the End of the Universe*

97. Assaulting those evil "compounds"!

I hope I'll always know when to swallow my pride and unabashedly borrow from the best. One of the very best, in terms of both witty writing and creative thinking, is Mike Kemp. I'll now step aside for a moment and let Mike have his very interesting say:

> Come on, folks — you know what a compound is. It's anyplace, including a plywood and tarpaper shack, where an "antigovernment whacko gun nut constitutionalist extremist" lives, particularly after the government has been informed that they AIN'T welcome on the place — and PARTICULARLY when government fails to believe it, and efforts are made to remove said whacko with, shall we say, extreme prejudice?

Just as a passing thought, has anyone noticed how government buildings...are constructed (or modified) these days? Parking lots have spots for "judges" or "elected officials" or "official vehicles" or "narcotics cars only." Surveillance cameras, metal detectors, checkpoints — you know, compounds.

First thing GOVERNMENT does, when they find a "compound," is cut off the electricity, telephone, gas, water. Gee! Is it that easy? Let's see... power and phone come in on wires on poles; if they are underground, most places, there is a convenient manhole, or some place where they come back to the surface somewhere nearby. Gas mains have big meters and a "Christmas tree" above ground; regulating and bypass stations; air conditioning plants have outside air intakes and heat exchangers; on site generators depend on diesel or gas trucked in from off-site. Water is ALWAYS piped in...

Double Gee Whiz! Do people LIVE in these compounds? Or do they drive cars to someplace else? To other compounds, with windows and burglar alarms and motion detectors and cell phones? And "security patrols" in the neighborhoods? With electric and phone wires, gas hookups, water mains...

Boy, the infrastructure is really vulnerable, ain't it? All those electric substations that feed designated portions of a town, sitting there aboveground? And those telephone junction boxes, at ground level? Natural gas "islands" with regulators and pumps? The only water supply for half of one city that I know of runs over a bridge in a big pipe right down the edge of a sidewalk.

And those cell phones operate in a fairly narrow bandwidth of modulated ultra high frequency... very high tech, but very vulnerable to some unprincipled tinkerer's dirty, unmodulated, high powered UHF jammer. Why, if somebody set one of those up, it would be like yelling SOOOOOIE at the trough — and nearly as easy as pushing a junker into a ditch on a country road and setting it on fire.

Once upon a time, the power company had a strike, that was quite drawn out, largely because there was not much deterioration in the system during the time period. However, there was a rash of trouble — ceramic insulators began to fail — seems as if they got in the way of a shower of copper-jacketed lead meteorites, and beavers began to attack creosoted poles. Strangest thing — slickest dern beavers you ever saw... make a cut flat enough to set a coke bottle on and not tip over. Left sawdust, too, not chips. This was a union town, and the union folks wouldn't pay their electric bills, in support of the strikers. Of course, there weren't many management types available, and those that did try to come around and cut off power got real discouraged from being met with bird guns and deer rifles... And when they got back to the office, they found a lot of cars and trucks with flat tires from all the bent sharpened and welded nails that had fallen in the parking lot. After the meteorite shower, and the beaver attack, that strike got settled faster than you could say "chain saw."

I offer my opponents a bargain: If they will stop telling lies about us, I will stop telling the truth about them. — Adlai Stevenson, campaign speech, 1952

98. Perfect disguise #2

Another way of hiding yourself in plain sight is to be so perfectly, boringly normal that no one notices you. You wear the same team's baseball cap everyone else wears, talk about the same TV shows, mow your lawn as religiously (or infrequently) as your neighbors, take your kids to McDonalds' Playplace, read the same pop novels, drink the same watery beer, and above all, express the same opinions as you'd arrive at if you'd taken the consensus of your neighbors. That is, if you express any opinions at all.

You never go to city council meetings or write red-hot le-ditors. You nod pleasantly but look conventionally guilty when a cop stops you for a traffic violation. And of course, you're driving a bronze Ford Taurus (or whatever else passes for normal in your location and income bracket) and have nothing on the seat but AAA maps and a Pizza Hut box. You attend PTA meetings, but look conventionally bored. You bowl, play tennis, or whatever your peers do, neither excelling nor flapping around like a wounded pterodactyl. You probably even have 2.3 children. Or 1.7 or whatever the number is right now. You are SO dull! And you do anything you want when nobody's looking. Or you don't do anything — except make plans.

You can even take your Normalcy Strategy to an interesting extreme by *being the kind of person you oppose*. One of my favorite Irish songs tells the story of such a person. He's Basil Brooke, a Protestant, Anglophilic Ulsterman so enamored of all things British he even papers the walls of his house in the colors of England's flag. Old Basil wears a bowler hat, marches in the Orangemen's parades and repeatedly declares: "Up the border, keep the border is me cry!" (Which roughly translates to: "Hooray for the border! Keep Ulster separate from the rest of Ireland.") At the end of the song, though, we learn Basil's actually working with *Sinn Fein* "...and the border will be blown up to the sky."

This is not to advocate "blowing up" anything. Not by any means! But old Basil does have a tricky and useful strategy. Hey, maybe something like that would even let *us* infiltrate *them* — a tactic they seem to think is very effective when worked the other way around. Wow, maybe you, too, can infiltrate a government supremacist group!

> *It's just another Sunday, in a tired old street.*
> *Police have got the chokehold, and we just lost the beat!*
> *Who counts the money underneath the bar?*
> *Who rides the wrecking ball into our guitars?*
> *Don't tell us you need us, 'cos we're just simple fools,*
> *Looking for America, coming through your schools. —*
> Starship, *We Built this City*

99. To the kids: Don't pay our debts

I was doing some research on an entirely different subject when I ran across this from an electronic magazine called *Profuse Discharge: Entrails of the Pepsi Generation*:

> We're the punks, phreaks, computer hackers, media terrorists, artists, writers, urban survivalists and comedians. We're the future, and we refuse to be a part of the past. ...

> The establishment is afraid of us, so it hates us and seeks to destroy us. The previous generation is convinced that we're just like they were and will end up being like them, and seek to push us in that path by removing the opportunities that they had, and that they, in turn, fucked up... If we go the way they want us to, we'll be paying their bills and spending the rest of our lives working our way out of the debt they landed us in. This isn't going to happen.

> This is our stand. This is where we say, "Fuck off" and be heard. This is the place where we're unchallenged. This is one of the places we're gaining momentum. We lost all respect for them, and now they have only formal control. We're tearing that away from them, too. We're individuals. We don't need them, and we sure as hell don't want them or their stupid ideals or their consumerism or their mentalities or their government. We want to be free. We want to take our chances and make it on our own, and we want to keep what we earn. We want to make our own world and build it on our own foundations and take our own chances at failing or succeeding. We're responsible for ourselves and we

watch out for each other, but we're not responsible for them. We're not responsible for each other. We believe in individual empowerment, not mass abdication to governments and corporations. That we're here and that we're gaining momentum is a clear indicator that we're succeeding and that they're failing miserably. Their society is collapsing, their government is failing, their businesses are folding, their control is rapidly crumbling and corrupting itself.

Message from the past (mine) to the future (yours): **More power to you, guys. Never give an inch!**

A few hundred million willing people in my generation — the Boomers — and a whole bunch more in my mama's generation, ran up a debt they're blandly expecting you to pay. The debt isn't just in money, as you are aware. The penalties, if you're foolish enough to accept them, will be beyond horror. Depression. Crime. Oppression. Hopelessness. Collapse of all you value. The money part alone is insanely awful, however. Officially, the federal government admits it has run up $6 trillion against your future. When you start counting in the "unfunded liabilities of the SS system and Medicare" that debt is actually *$17 trillion or more* — because nobody knows what the health care of the future is going to cost. It's a blank check they expect you to sign.

You're right. *Don't pay it.* You didn't incur that planet-sized debt. You didn't agree to it. And you, the writer of the angry screed above and your friends, are under *no* obligation to a bunch of politicians and ponzi scheme beneficiaries who thought they could carelessly waste your future on their own momentary, entirely illusory, security. It would be better for your generation to let mine starve in the streets than for you to allow knaves to impose their vice and folly on yet one more generation. Ponzi scheme promoters and participants don't deserve to be rescued from the consequences of their foolery. Yes. Don't pay. Stop. Rebel. Refuse. Tell the knaves of my generation to reap the logical consequences of their reality evasions. Tell them that to be fully human and free means facing reality.

The money is only the smallest part of this attempted intergenerational crime. And you know it, don't you? They have forced you to make a hard, wrenching choice between being full, free human beings or mere cattle to be milked by wrinkled old hands. The politicians and their followers, which probably include most of your parents, their friends, your teachers, your counselors, your cops, your ministers, your neighbors, don't just want you to pay in money for their indulgences. They have ridden you with laws, stolen your opportunities, made your pleasures illegal, tried to herd your wild, young thoughts into politically correct corrals, limited your options, shortened your horizons and generally tried to forbid you from becoming fully, wonderfully uniquely human.

Don't let them get away with it. Don't let *us* get away with it, to whatever extent we individuals of my generation tried to do this to you for our own sakes. Those of our generation who have a shred of integrity, a shred of real decency, will take care of ourselves and, to whatever extent we can, take care of the Ponzi schemers. You take care of yourselves — and the future of free humanity.

Boomers, read it again:

> We're responsible for ourselves and we watch out for each other, but we're not responsible for them. We're not responsible for each other. We believe in individual empowerment, not mass abdication to governments and corporations.

Read it and fear for the fools of our generation.

You think it won't come to pass? You think these kids will become just like millions of our contemporaries? You think they'll knuckle under and become good sheep-izens? The writer of *Profuse Discharge* knows you may think that. He's heard exactly what we heard from our parents. Most of our parents turned out to be exactly right. But maybe... maybe... this time it won't happen. This time a generation might fulfill its own bitter potential — not because they are more determined than we were, but because we may have left them *no other option*. They might not have the chance to follow the Boomers into complacency, even if they someday want to. The thieves in our ranks may simply have stolen so much from their generation that there's nothing left to take, and nothing the angry young will be willing to give, nothing they will allow to be wrenched from them without mortal resistance or adamant, eternal refusal. And more power to them.

More power to you, you pissed off, outraged, robbed, cheated, lied to free young rebels. Be as decent and humane as your nature, your hopes and your fury will allow. But for God's sake and your own and the sake of all hopes, don't let us cast our generation's chains around your humanity

> *There is no "thin blue line," only a deep red stream — the productive class — that cops and crooks wade through alike, without a thought or care to the lives, liberties, or property of those they're destroying.* — L. Neil Smith (Mirelle Stein, *The Productive Class*), Pallas

100. Uncle Howard, Niels Bohr and salvaging what you can

Despite mild reform of federal civil asset forfeiture laws, and despite the very hopeful 1998 law that put the burden of proof in tax matters on the IRS, confiscation of property remains — and always will remain — a dire problem under unjust governments.

It's bad enough now. It will get worse. Someday, you may have to flee for your life. Maybe you'll have to give up everything in order to take your last, flying chance at freedom. Or someday, you may have to put up with stormtroopers smashing through your home in search of "contraband." You'll need to find desperately clever ways to outwit them. You want to scrounge and salvage something... anything... out of the chaos. In those times, it might help to listen to the experiences of a handful of survivors, glowing out of the darkness of the Nazi occupation.

First, Jim Davidson, chairman of Interglobal Paratronics, Inc., tells this story of an old friend of his family:

> My mother's roommate in college married a nice Jewish boy who came to be known to my brothers and me as "Uncle Howard." Uncle Howard's parents came from Germany with him when he was just a little boy.
>
> It was 1937, and the Nazis were letting people leave, but only if they left their valuables behind. If you tried to get over the border with artwork, gold, jewelry, it was all seized. Now, Uncle Howard's father had a good bit of money. They drove a nice Mercedes touring sedan. In the "boot" it had a toolbox. The old man dumped the tools out and took them, along with all his wealth in cash, to a Jewish friend in the jewelry business. His friend used the tools to make molds. He used all the money (less commission and fee) to buy platinum. Then he cast a brand new set of auto repair tools

out of pure platinum. No finish was applied, so they had a dull sheen.

Then the family was loaded up in the car. Howard's mother and sisters wore some jewelry, so the border guards would have something to confiscate. Howard's dad had some cash to let them confiscate. Other than that, they just had clothes and a few books, a Torah, and their lives. Oh, yeah, and about $8 million U.S. in platinum tools in the trunk. They drove to Switzerland. Things at the border proceeded as expected. The Nazis confiscated about 200,000 Marks in cash and jewelry. And the family escaped with its fortune intact.

Perhaps one of the nicest bits of hitherto unpublished smuggling. Something to keep in mind because the attitude of, "It could never happen here," makes it more likely that it will.[3]

And then there is the story of physicist Niels Bohr. Bohr was in Denmark when the Nazis occupied the country. To prevent them from confiscating Nobel Prize gold medals entrusted to him by two other scientists. He *dissolved them*, and kept the gold salts in a *mis-labeled bottle*. The literal-minded Nazis would never have had a clue.

The literal-mindedness of tyrants is as important to keep in mind as their greed. Even in less dire circumstances than Bohr's or Uncle Howard's, it's often possible to "hide things

---

[3] When I ran this item by Jim just prior to publication, he wryly warned me that Uncle Howard was occasionally known to "file the serial numbers" off other people's stories and use them as his own. So the story is probably true, but whether it is truly Howard's is another matter. However, Jim also told me of a contemporary American (this story verifiable) who, in the dark pre-1973 days when it was a "crime" to own gold, used to drive into the U.S. across the Mexican border in a car featuring solid gold (but carefully painted) hubcaps. Good old American ingenuity. I love it!

in plain sight" or give the rapacious agents of the state an easy object to seize while preserving more important assets.

I know one young man, for instance, who was an automatic target for the IRS because of his unusually high pay and the equally unusual terms on which he received it. Every year, year after year, he was audited. After a couple of years, he figured out that if he simply gave the auditors *one, huge, obvious thing to "find,"* they'd grab that — and miss much more subtle, but much larger, tricks he pulled to retain possession of his earnings. A favorite was taking a large deduction for "uniforms." The IRS knew darned well that a high-priced consultant didn't wear "uniforms." When they "caught him" making this iffy claim, the young man would indignantly explain that, "The only time I ever wear my three-piece suits is for work! So of course they're a uniform!" The auditor would, with equal indignation and glee, disallow the deduction, levy interest and penalties, and demand the $3,000 or $4,000 — that the young man had already set aside for that purpose. And every year, year after year, the young man would "get away" with a great deal more. I wouldn't have believed it, but I know him and I know his honesty (when dealing with honest people) and I personally observed him practicing this ruse. And it worked. If you or I were an IRS auditor, we might figure that one fishy deduction would probably be a sign of others. But then, you and I are more creative than your average Nazi border guard or IRS auditor.

Here's one final story from the dark era of the Nazis, which demonstrates that even something as simple as innocent honesty can baffle a tyrant, who expects deception. This one is from Corrie Ten Boom's moving book, *The Hiding Place.*

The Ten Boom family was passionately active trying to save the Jews of Holland, coordinating an entire network of hiding places within old and complex city houses. They were, however, terribly worried about the refugees hidden in the home of one relative. The relative's problem: She was incapable of lying. Everyone was terrified that, if the Nazis raided her house, she would simply tell them where the Jews were. And she did. When the stormtroopers burst into her home one day at dinnertime and demanded to know where the Jews were concealed, she pointed under the table in mute terror. She was telling them exactly where the Jews were — in a chamber under the floorboards, reached by a trap door. But the literal-minded Nazis, expecting deception, thought the woman was mocking them by pretending a whole houseful of Jewish refugees was *crouched under the tablecloth*. So, in rage and contempt, they stormed the whole house — without looking in the one spot to which she had pointed.

Yes, today, there are technologies that enable even mindless thugs to detect warm bodies or hidden metals. That much has changed. But the mindset hasn't. We can, with a will and some good fortune, outwit any thug or tyrant on the planet and salvage a bit of our own lives.

> *I see the clouds which now rise thick and fast upon our horizon, the thunder roll, and the lightning play, and to that God who rides the whirlwind and directs the storm, I submit my country.* — Josiah Quincy, December 16, 1773, moments before the Boston Tea Party

101. "...like a fish in water."

Mao Zedong taught, "A guerrilla must move among the people like a fish in water." I don't make a habit of quoting

Chairman Mao, but when a friend tossed out this quote yesterday, I knew immediately it not only belonged in this book, but in some important spot.

The moment we opted out of "the system" we became guerrillas. This doesn't mean we picked up our guns and hit the jungles. It means we became partisans for freedom who have chosen to stand for freedom from outside the institutions the tyrants control. Whether we operate in forests, deserts, urban jungles or university corridors, we are inherently outsiders now. And we are in a fight — for something far more important than our mere lives.

So what does it mean for a guerrilla to move among the people like a fish in water? At first blush, one might say it simply means to move as smoothly and quietly as possible through society, not calling undue attention to our activities. That's a good idea, where possible. But on a more fundamental level, it means that we *need* the people among whom we move. We need them for our very survival, as a fish needs water. We need them to surround us and nurture us. And we must respect them for that, even when we have no respect at all for what they believe or how they choose to live. It means, when the time for danger is upon us, that we must never treat the lives of our neighbors and other non-combatants as expendable.

For their sake...

Occasionally, I hear some person who presents himself as a military strategy guru dismissing deaths of innocents as "collateral damage." Such dispassionate "experts" treat those deaths as necessary and insignificant. Bull-ony. It's damn significant to the individuals it happens to. And to the people who love them.

We must never aggress against innocents. If we do, then we're precisely as bad as the people we claim to be opposing, and for the same reason — lack of respect for individual rights and individual lives. Whatever jerk thought it was okay to kill babies and credit union customers in order to strike at the fedgov at the Murrah Building was a collectivist pig as filthy as any in Washington, D.C. (Not to mention the likelihood that the person who made the decision may have *been* someone in Washington, D.C., if the bombing was a runaway federal sting or a Reichstag fire, as evidence indicates.) That group-thinking person was making a decision that individuals don't matter. But individuals do matter. More than anything. Even the individuals some of us call sheeple. Even the ones we might better term by the old corporate joke, mushrooms — folks who are kept in the dark and fed shit. Some of those people may suffer and die when hard times hit. And we may be neither able nor willing to do anything for them as they suffer the consequences of their own blind choices. But we have no right whatsoever to do anything *to* them. We must not aggress against them. For their sake...

And for ours.

If you think all this is just idealistic, mushy-hearted philosophizing, let's go back to the very practical military strategist, Mao. One reason *he* thought his guerrillas should move like fish in water was what I mentioned earlier; their own survival. And their own success as guerrillas. Someday, we might need these folks to feed us, shelter us, hide us, and carry us to places of safety. They're only going to do that if they perceive us as being on their side. Part of their world.

Right now, of course, they don't and they wouldn't. The freedom movement has been so successfully demonized the average American probably believes everyone who opposes uncontrolled government is an uneducated, pot-bellied, racist, gun-nut (Well, they're right about the gun-nut part.), mean-spirited, macho, about-to-go-postal loner whacko who spends his spare time blowing up churches and, horror of horrors, would wear cammies to his grandmother's tea party.

They also see us, probably rightly, as a threat to all the layers of "security" with which they've allowed the governments of the country to surround them. Within their security blankets, they're warm, but out of touch. They're "safe," but they've forgotten there's something called freedom that's awesome beyond anything a safety addict can understand. All they know is that by threatening to take away the power of Big Government, we threaten to take away all their little "benefits," all that makes life easy for them, all that enables them to live numb, unseeing and uncommitted.

Maybe that'll always be the case. And if so, we can never count on ordinary people to aid us. On the other hand, with both government and media rapidly losing respect, we could have a turnaround in that view at any time. And *if* the hard times to come involve a drying up of the nannygov's teat, millions might turn against government and its propagandistic media as thoroughly as they once depended upon them. It's hard to say. But we should watch for any such opportunity.

Even if there's never a large scale revulsion against an American tyranny, there will still be tiny pockets of ordinary people who *will* help us — if we let them. These may be relatives and neighbors who'll help us just because their loyalties lie in relationships. These may be people who just get a thrill out of something vaguely illicit. They may be soft-hearted grannies (and granpas) who'd take us in as if we were wounded kitties. Or they may be people who've been pissed at government all along, but have just never seen any reason to act — until they perceive freedom-fighting Americans to be threatened. But these people *won't* help us — and we won't deserve help — if we attack them or people they perceive to be like themselves. They won't help if they see us acting with gratuitous violence.

There are ways not only to keep from alienating them, but to win them to our side. In some guerrilla campaigns in poorer countries than ours, the fighters have gone so far as to establish soup kitchens and schools to help the people around them. I have a hard time picturing most of us doing that. (Although I can see my LDS freedom-fighting friends and a few others doing it.) And, not being a third-world country at the moment, our needs are different, anyway.

But it's really simple. If we regard the people around us as expendable — or as too unimportant to worry about — then think about how they're going to regard us. And they outnumber us. Keep the moral high ground, always. If killing ever becomes necessary — and pray that it does not — save your killing fury for those who've earned it. Operate for freedom with a scalpel, not a chain saw; a carefully targeted arrow, not a bomb.

Afterword:
Why this book is dedicated to Wat Tyler

On June 7, 1381, peasants in the south of England rose in rebellion. Jean Froissart's *Chronicles*, a contemporary history, explains:

> It is the custom in England, as in several other countries, for the nobles to have strong powers over their men and to hold them in serfdom... In England there is much greater number than elsewhere of such men who are obliged to serve the prelates and the nobles. And in the countries of Kent, Essex, Sussex and Bedford in particular, there are more than in the whole of the rest of England.

> These bad people in the counties just mentioned began to rebel because, they said, they were held too much in subjection...and they were treated like animals. This was a thing they could no longer endure, wishing rather to be all one and the same... In these machinations they had been greatly encouraged originally by a priest of Kent called John Ball who [preached] thus:

> "Good people, ...in what way are those whom we call lords greater masters than ourselves? How have they

deserved it? Why do they hold us in bondage? If we all spring from a single father and mother, Adam and Eve, how can they claim or prove that they are lords more than us, except by making us produce and grow the wealth which they spend? ...From us must come, from our labor, the things which keep them in luxury. We are called serfs and beaten if we are slow in our service to them, yet we have no sovereign lord we can complain to, none to hear us and do us justice. Let us go to the king — he is young — and show him how we are oppressed, and tell him that we want things to be changed, or else we will change them ourselves. If we go in good earnest and all together, very many people who are called serfs and are held in subjection will follow us to get their freedom. And when the king sees and hears us, he will remedy the evil, either willingly or otherwise."

....The things [Ball] was doing and saying came to the ears of the common people of London, who were envious of the nobles and rich. These began saying that the country was badly governed and was being robbed of its wealth by those who called themselves noblemen. So these wicked men in London started to become disaffected and to rebel and they sent word to the people in the counties mentioned to come boldly to London with all their followers, when they would find the city open and the common people on their side. They could then so work on the King that there would be no more serfs in England.

These promises incited the people of Kent, Essex, Sussex, Bedford and the neighboring districts and they set off and went towards London. They were a full sixty thousand and their chief captain was one Wat Tyler. With him as his companions were Jack Straw and John Ball. These three were the leaders and Wat Tyler was the greatest of them. He was a tiler of roofs, and a wicked and nasty fellow he was...

On June 7, the peasants began their march, burning the homes of lawyers and judges along the way. According to the *Encyclopedia Britannica* (1997 CD ROM edition):

> Tyler led them in the capture of Canterbury (June 10); of the Savoy palace belonging to John of Gaunt, the King's uncle (June 13); and of London Bridge and the Tower of London (June 14). Although King Richard II promised concessions on June 14, Tyler's men refused to disarm and disband. They met with Richard on June 15 at Smithfield, where Tyler presented more radical demands...

According to another contemporary chronicler (quoted in Charles Oman, *The Great Revolt of 1381*, Oxford: Clarendon Press, 1906), the demands and the king's response were thus:

> The King asked him what were the points which he wished to have revised, and he should have them freely, without contradiction, written out and sealed. Thereupon the said Walter rehearsed the points which were to be demanded; and he asked that there should be no law within the realm save the law of Winchester, and that from henceforth there should be no outlawry in any process of law, and that no lord should have lordship save civilly, and that there should be equality among all people save only the King... And he demanded that there should be no more villeins in England, and no serfdom or villeinage, but that all men should be free and of one condition. To this the King gave an easy answer, and said that he should have all that he could fairly grant, reserving only for himself the regality of his crown. And then he bade him go back to his home, without making further delay.

As the king made his easy promises, however, a scuffle broke out between Tyler and members of the king's retinue. A mortally wounded Tyler was carried to St. Bartholomew's Hospital, but he wasn't to die there. The Lord Mayor of

London ordered him dragged out before the rebels and beheaded. The chronicler continues:

> And when the commons saw that their chieftain, Wat Tyler, was dead in such a manner, they fell to the ground there among the wheat, like beaten men, imploring the King for mercy for their misdeeds. And the King benevolently granted them mercy, and most of them took to flight....

> Afterwards the King sent out his messengers into divers parts, to capture the malefactors and put them to death. And many were taken and hanged at London, and they set up many gallows around the City of London, and in other cities and boroughs of the south country. At last, as it pleased God, the King... took pity in his heart, and granted them all pardon, on condition that they should never rise again, under pain of losing life or members, and that *each of them should get his charter of pardon, and pay the King as fee for his seal twenty shillings, to make him rich.* And so finished this wicked war.

Other Books of Interest:

☐ **94281 101 THINGS TO DO 'TIL THE REVOLUTION, Ideas and resources for self-liberation, monkey wrenching and preparedness,** *by Claire Wolfe.* We don't need a weatherman to know which way the wind blows — but we do need the likes of Claire Wolfe, whose book offers 101 suggestions to help grease the wheels as we roll towards the government's inevitable collapse. "Kill your TV... Join a gun-rights group... Fly the Gadsden flag... Buy and carry the Citizens' Rule Book... Join the tax protesters on April 15... Bury gold, guns, and goodies..." Wolfe's list is lengthy and thought-provoking, as she elaborates on each piece of advice, from generalities to precise instructions. For the concerned citizen who wishes to keep a low profile, protect his or her rights, and survive in the "interesting times" which are sure to come, this is essential reading. *1996, 5½ x 8½, 225 pp, soft cover.* $15. 95.

☐ **14177 COMMUNITY TECHNOLOGY,** *by Karl Hess, With an introduction by Carol Moore.* In the 1970s, the late Karl Hess participated in a five-year social experiment in Washington, D.C.'s Adams-Morgan neighborhood. Hess and several thousand others labored to make their neighborhood as self-sufficient as possible, turning to such innovative techniques as raising fish in basements, growing contained bacteriological toilets, and planning a methanol plant to convert garbage to fuel. There was a newsletter and weekly community meetings, giving Hess and others a taste of participatory government that changed their lives forever. *1979, 5½ x 8½, 120 pp, soft cover.* $9.95.

☐ **10067 BULLETPROOF PRIVACY, How to Live Hidden, Happy, and Free!,** *by Boston T. Party.* This book explains how to maintain any level or degree of privacy that the reader desires. While many of the other privacy books are outdated or just plain fluffy, *Bulletproof Privacy* is a street-savvy digest compiled by a practicing expert. The author has maintained a low profile all over the world, and his knowledge, insight, and mastery of prose, interwoven with his clear witty style make this book the modern definitive guide in these troubled times. *1997, 5½ x 8½, 160 pp, soft cover.* $16.00.

☐ **76054 YOU & THE POLICE!,** *by Boston T. Party.* Have you ever felt abused by the police when merely going about your lawful business? Have you ever been intimidated by a cop, and didn't really know how to handle it? Have you ever wanted to reserve your rights, but weren't sure exactly how to do so? Well, if you don't know your rights, you never really had any rights! This is the book for any American citizen who wants to know and defend his rights when dealing with the police. This high-spirited little manual covers everything you need to protect yourself. *1996, 5½ x 8½, 125 pp, illustrated, soft cover.* $15.00.

☐ **58095 THE POLICEMAN IS YOUR FRIEND AND OTHER LIES,** *by Ned Beaumont.* America is a society built upon lies, supported by lies, and dedicated to promoting lies. In this astounding revealing look at the deceptions that are perpetrated upon us from infancy to old age, author Ned Beaumont peels away the fabric of deception and unveils the hidden untruths that enslave us and poison our perceptions. Policemen, bureaucrats, teachers, politicians, lawyers, financiers, military leaders — they are all part of the system that distorts our most basic freedoms and beliefs, and molds us into unthinking minions of the entrenched power structure. *1996, 5½ x 8½, 160 pp, soft cover.* $14.95.

☐ **10065 HOW TO HIDE THINGS IN PUBLIC PLACES,** *by Dennis Fiery.* Did you ever want to hide something from prying eyes, yet were afraid to do so in your home? Now you can secrete your valuables away from home, by following the eye-opening instructions contained in this book, which identifies many of the public cubbyholes and niches that can be safely employed for this purpose. Absolutely the finest book ever written on the techniques involved in hiding your possessions in public. *1996, 5½ x 8½, 220 pp, illustrated, soft cover.* $15. 00.

☐ **10060 OUR VANISHING PRIVACY, And What You Can Do To Protect Yours,** *by Robert Ellis Smith.* This shocking book reveals how much strangers know about your private life. Someone's collecting information about your health, your finances, your love life. And they don't have your best interests at heart. This book reveals the secrets of the snoops, what they know and how they get their information, and tells you what you need to know to fight back. *1993, 5½ x 8½, 136 pp, soft cover.* $12.95.

☐ **19197 STREET SMARTS FOR THE NEW MILLENNIUM,** *by Jack Luger.* Life can be risky for the average citizen. There are criminal elements in our society, as well as pitfalls in our everyday life, which pose real dangers to the safety and security of ourselves and our families. In this unique book, author Jack Luger has provided the methods and resources that enable the reader to minimize these threats to our lives, liberties, and pursuit of happiness. So don't be a victim! Learn to be self reliant, and arm yourself with the knowledge that it takes to develop your street smarts and survive this dangerous decade! *1996, 5½ x 8½, 138 pp, soft cover.* $15.00.

☐ **14187 HOW TO LIVE WITHOUT ELECTRICITY — AND LIKE IT,** *by Anita Evangelista.* There's no need to remain dependent on commercial electrical systems for your home's comforts and security. This book describes many alternative methods that can help one become more self-reliant and free from the utility companies. Learn how to light, heat and cool your home, obtain and store water, cook and refrigerate food, and fulfill many other household needs without paying the power company! *1997, 5½ x 8½, 168 pp, illustrated, soft cover.* $13.95.

☐ **14176 HOW TO DEVELOP A LOW-COST FAMILY-FOOD STORAGE SYSTEM,** *by Anita Evangelista.* If you're weary of spending a large percentage of your income on your family's food needs, then you should follow this amazing book's numerous tips on food-storage techniques. Slash your food bill by over fifty percent, and increase your self-sufficiency at the same time through alternative ways of obtaining, processing and storing foodstuffs. Includes methods of freezing, canning, smoking, salting, pickling, drying, and many other food-preservation procedures. *1995, 5½ x 8½, 120 pp, illustrated, indexed, soft cover.* $10.00.

☐ **14193 BACKYARD MEAT PRODUCTION,** *by Anita Evangelista.* If you're tired of paying ever-soaring meat prices, and worried about unhealthy food additives and shoddy butchering techniques, then you should start raising small meat-producing animals at home! You needn't live in the country, as most urban areas allow for this practice. This book clearly explains how to raise rabbits, chickens, quail, pheasants, guineas, ducks, and mini-goats and –pigs for their meat and by-products, which can not only be consumed but can also be sold or bartered to specialized markets. Improve your diet while saving money and becoming more self-sufficient! *1997, 5½ x 8½, 136 pp, illustrated, soft cover.* $14.95.

☐ **70050 PIRATE RADIO OPERATIONS,** *by Andrew Yoder and Earl T. Gray.* Pirate radio is one of the Communication Age's most fascinating developments! Now, for those hobbyists who yearn to learn the ins and outs of clandestine radio broadcasting, there's a wealth of knowledge available in *Pirate Radio Operations!* For the first time, there's a hands-on manual that fully explains the intricacies of this burgeoning pastime. Yoder has devoted his energies to pirate radio for years, and now he shares his practical expertise with the world. Complete with numerous photographs and illustrations that provide workable designs and schematics for all pirate radio buffs, this is the finest how-to book ever published on this subject. *1997, 5½ x 8½, 364 pp, illustrated, soft cover.* **$19.95.**

☐ **94068 NATIVE AMERICAN ANARCHISM,** *by Eunice Minette Schuster.* The history of anarchism in the United States from colonial times to the early 20th Century. Covers the abolitionists; women's rights movements; supporters of reproductive and sexual freedom; pacifist and anti-war movements; alternative communities and much more. *1932, 5½ x 8½, 202 pp, indexed, bibliography, soft cover.* **$12.00.**

☐ **94067 THE MYTH OF NATURAL RIGHTS,** *by L.A. Rollins.* In this seminal work, L.A. Rollins effectively demolishes the myth of "natural rights." He exposes the "bleeding heart libertarians" who promote these rights, including Ayn Rand, Murray Rothbard, Tibor Machan, Samuel Konkin and others. Rollins dissects the arguments for natural rights, cutting through the faulty logic to the core of libertarian dogma. An important book for libertarians who take their ideas seriously. *1983, 5½ x 8½, 50 pp, bibliography, soft cover.* **$7.95.**

☐ **94101 NATURAL LAW, or Don't Put a Rubber on Your Willie,** *by Robert Anton Wilson.* A continuing episode in the critique of natural rights theories started by L.A. Rollins' *The Myth of Natural Rights,* Wilson lets fly at Murray Rothbard, George Smith, Samuel Konkin and other purveyors of the "claim that some sort of metaphysical entity called a 'right' resides in a human being like a 'ghost' residing in a haunted house." An entertaining, informative and well-thought-out book that should be read by anyone who has ever been attracted by an ideology. *1987, 5½ x 8½, 72 pp, soft cover.* **$7.95.**

To order any of the above titles, please use the order form on the next page. If you are ordering with a Visa, Discover, or Mastercard you can call our toll-free number 1-800-380-2230, 24 hours a day, 7 days a week.

- ☐ 94281 101 Things to do 'Til the Revolution, $15.95
- ☐ 14177 Community Technology, $9.95
- ☐ 10067 Bulletproof Privacy, $16.00
- ☐ 76054 You & The Police, $15.00
- ☐ 58095 The Policeman Is Your Friend, $14.95
- ☐ 10065 How To Hide Things In Public Places, $15.00
- ☐ 10060 Our Vanishing Privacy, $12.95
- ☐ 19197 Street Smarts for the New Millennium, $15.00
- ☐ 14187 How To Live Without Electricity — And Like It, $13.95
- ☐ 14176 How To Develop a Low-Cost Family-Food Storage System, $10.00
- ☐ 14193 Backyard Meat Production, $14.95
- ☐ 70050 Pirate Radio Operations, $19.95
- ☐ 94068 Native American Anarchism, $12.00
- ☐ 94067 The Myth of Natural Rights, $7.95
- ☐ 94101 Natural Law, $7.95
- ☐ 88888 2002 Main Catalog

Loompanics Unlimited
PO Box 1197
Port Townsend, WA 98368

Shoot202

Please send me the books I have checked above. I have enclosed $_____ which includes $5.95 for shipping and handling of the first $25.00 ordered. Add an additional $1 shipping for each additional $25 ordered. Washington residents include 8.3% sales tax.

Name _____

Address _____

City/State/Zip_____

VISA, Discover, and MasterCard accepted.
Call 1-800-380-2230 for credit card orders *only,*
24 hours a day, 7 days a week
Check out our website: www.loompanics.com
Turn to the next page for our catalog ad.